A THOUSAND TRAILS

A THOUSAND TRAILS

Hugh Steven

The personal journal of
William Cameron Townsend
1917-1919

CREDO Publishing Corporation
#202, 15261 Russell Avenue
White Rock, British Columbia V4B 2P7

ISBN 0-920479-00-6 (paperback)

CREDO Publishing Corporation
#202, 15261 Russell Avenue
White Rock, British Columbia V4B 2P7
Printed in the United States of America

Dedicated to:

Elaine Townsend
and the family–
Grace
Joy
Elainadel
Bill

This is love; not that we have loved God, but that he loved us and sent his Son as an atoning sacrifice for our sins. Dear friends, since God loved us, we ought to love one another.

John, the beloved Disciple
(I John 4:10-11)

I have come to realize that it is imperative this need be surmounted in this generation and the people be reached with the message of salvation.

William Cameron
Townsend,
age 22, Guatemala, 1918

Love the Lord your God with all your heart and with all your mind. This is the first and greatest commandment. And the second is like it; love your neighbor as yourself.

Jesus Christ, God's Son
(Matthew 22:37)

Those who attain to any excellence commonly spend life in some single pursuit, for excellence is not gained upon easier terms.

Johnson

You may have thousands of guardians in your Christian life; you have only one father. For it was I who through the gospel became your father in the Christian faith. I therefore appeal to you to take me as your pattern and example.

Paul, the Apostle
(I Corinthians 4:15, 16)

God has given me youthful vigor, faith and a challenge. Therefore I have decided to devote my life to the evangelization of the Indian people.

William Cameron
Townsend,
age 22, Guatemala, 1918

Contents

Acknowledgements

Born out of many years of close association with Mr. Townsend, Dr. Benjamin Elson volunteered to read the beginning manuscript and offer me his own unique perspective on the life and times of Cameron Townsend. I here thank him for his insight, as well as Dr. Richard Pittman, who like Dr. Elson is a longtime colleague, friend and confidante. Dr. Pittman has made his own significant contribution to the world of Wycliffe by producing *One Ship Sails East* and *Remember all the Way*. I'm grateful for the use of some of these materials in this biography.

For many years Calvin Hibbard served Mr. Townsend as his personal secretary. Currently he functions as archivist for the Townsend papers. It was he who efficiently and graciously assisted in securing the early personal correspondence and photographs. Mrs. Anna Marie Dahlquist, Rev. Paul Burgess's maternal granddaughter, provided eleventh-hour and previously unknown letters that were invaluable in gaining a greater perspective into the life of Elvira Malmstrom.

I offer special appreciation to Elaine Townsend who read the manuscript and has given me her lovely God-given gift of encouragement to continue with a second volume of Cam's memoirs. My typist Valarie Sluss deserves credit for retaining her good humor, sanity and eyesight while struggling with my impossible scrawled-up drafts. I'm especially grateful for my daughter-in-law Kristi Steven who, when given a time limit, typed the final corrections in record time. I thank my wife Norma who as a writer and editor in her own right deserves greater credit than she publicly receives for her steadfast love and skill in assisting me in bringing life and order to the printed page.

A special note of thanks must go to Mr. Anthony Rossi, a dear friend of the Townsends for his special assistance in the publication of this book.

I also thank Wycliffe Associates for choosing to celebrate Wycliffe's 50th anniversary by endorsing this book as their tribute to the memory of William Cameron Townsend.

Finally, I acknowledge my deep appreciation to Ethel Wallis, longtime Wycliffe colleague, friend and enthusiastic mentor for first bringing my attention to Mr. Townsend's journal, *A Thousand Trails*. While browsing her way through the SIL library at Norman, Oklahoma one summer, she "accidentally" discovered a yellowed dog-eared manuscript. Said Ethel, "When I picked it up and began to leaf my way through it, I knew it was pure gold!"

Introduction

"I here examine the past to consider the future."

One function of literature is to remind us of the beautiful things we have forgotten. Therefore, in the interest of history, and in the interest of remembering the "beautiful" things William Cameron Townsend accomplished during his lifetime, I here present a compilation of a previously unpublished journal, his diary and letters written in Central America between the years 1917 to 1919.

As you read this account you might experience a kind of *déjà vu,* as if you've read some of this before. If you have been a reader of the New Testament, particularly of Acts, you have indeed read it before! Without realizing it, Cameron Townsend, at age twenty-one, lived out a scenario similar to the Apostle Paul nineteen centuries before him. Was it for this reason that Dr. Kenneth L. Pike, President Emeritus of the Summer Institute of Linguistics and candidate for the Nobel Peace Prize, called Cameron Townsend one of the greatest and most creative men since the Apostle Paul? Note the following from Townsend's diary:

> I had the feeling the Lord wanted us to stay all night at the last settlement and teach more instead of hurrying through. Accordingly, we followed the trail back five miles to the settlement. There I stayed at the home of the man whom the Lord had put on my heart, explaining the way of salvation.

Other Pauline similarities come from Cam's numerous encounters with mobs, police and jails, and in journeyings over long, hot trails and mountains; through tropical rainstorms, mud and swamps; battling mosquitoes, ticks and bugs of every description, and often with "nothing to eat but a single tortilla and some tepid water."

Yet, as you read this account, you come to understand why God wanted this young man to experience such hardship. He was to, one day, pioneer an organization that would require most of the young people who joined him to also experience long, hard, hot and lonely trails, and because he experienced such prolonged and extended hiking and trail chomping, he could therefore quite properly ask each of the young people who joined the organization to do the same. He had been there first.

Another insight is that here was a man of grand contradictions. He was a man of his times, yet he did not surrender to rules of conformity. Townsend's diary reveals early evidence of his openness, spontaneity and creativity; an explorer who chose not to follow existing models. Juxtaposed to this was a young man with a no-nonsens straightforward faith and commitment to Jesus Christ; a man who possessed noble ideas and an inner vision to reach the world's bypassed peoples for God through the Scriptures.

It was this faith, this vision, this singlemindedness, that became Cameron Townsend's hallmark, and it came from a settled conviction about why he had been created. He was a man at peace with himself, who knew he was appropriately placed in the scheme of God's will. Thus when he believed a certain course of action was God-directed, he acted, never doubting. Like the Apostle Paul, Mr. Townsend was fully persuaded that God had the power to do what He had promised (Romans 4:21). Later, God called him to Bible translation, and he knew it. Nevermind his illnesses and lack of formal higher education. Nevermind the discouragement he received for using the Cakchiquel language over Spanish as the medium of instruction for the two hundred thousand Cakchiquel people. William Cameron Townsend knew God; his mind was at rest. He forthrightly forged ahead believing God was guiding his dreams.

While his confidence was in God, not men, Cameron knew how to use the resources at his disposal. In fact, when a man once challenged him about what was, in this man's judgment, an excessive use of "methods," Cam said, "God expects us to use the means, but the One who acts and will use it for us is the Lord Himself. Just as Christ used temporal things – water, fish, bread – to perform miracles, so we too use temporal tools to accomplish our task. The difference is, our confidence is always in the Lord, not in the tool." Cam's view of God was simply that God was the One who integrates everything that exists for His own purposes.

An important distinction of Cam's life is found in Psalm 16:8, "I have set the Lord always before me. Because he is at my right hand, I will not be shaken."

Yet while Cameron Townsend knew exactly who he served, who the enemy was, what he wanted and where he was going, he was a deeply human man. He smiled easily and told little jokes on himself (never on his colleagues). He enjoyed a party and became famous for his love of cherry pie. It was he who coined the phrase, "Let's put as much 'pie' in pioneering as possible!"

Cam was the kind of man who took time – often out of impossible schedules and heavy demands – to consistently communicate with his friends by telephone, letter and personal visits. By a God-given instinct and obedience to the Scriptures that exhort all believers to be hospitable and sincerely friendly, Cam was a friend to all, no matter what their station or rank. Cam knew that to be a friend and to maintain friendship required costly energy. By example he taught us all how to be a true friend: "By love serve one another."

That Cam was a man who took time to smell the flowers is evidenced by all who knew him, and it began early in his life:

> I came upon an alligator and watched him swimming awhile before he noticed me...

> I threw some rocks at an armadillo. Only his armor saved him...

I have no idea if the Apostle Paul ever tossed a stone at an armadillo. I do know, however, that Paul walked great distances on his first missionary journey, and so did Mr. Townsend. As he describes in his journal, "I walked a thousand trails, all different, throughout Guatemala, Honduras, El Salvador and Nicaragua in an effort to introduce people to Jesus Christ, my Lord."

The vision that began in 1917 has spread over six decades to enthuse, capture and motivate hundreds of men and women who believe, as did Cameron Townsend, that the Christian mandate is to "go into the world and preach the gospel to every creature." That this is true is reflected in the two world-wide organizations he founded – Wycliffe Bible Translators (WBT) and the Summer Institute of Linguistics (SIL).

For those who knew him, there was no evidence of the slackening of his vision; no contrast between the aspirations of youth and the attainment of age; no decay of imagination or passion for the forgotten person without the Scriptures in his own language. On his deathbed in April 1982, Cameron

Townsend was still suggesting and outlining the direction he wanted the two organizations to take.

Cameron Townsend was not a perfect man. He had faults and at times exasperated some of his friends and colleagues. Said one critic, "He was a man with only one vision; a kind of one-dimensional man." Said another, "He was a visionary extraordinaire." Whatever he was (and history will reveal this), he was a man of remarkable moral leadership and courage. The same day he learned of Chet Bitterman's assassination, he flew to Colombia to offer his special brand of encouragement and help to SIL Colombia branch members. He was over eighty.

In a way, what he did in Colombia he had done all his life for his friends and the Wycliffe family – he was living out the principles of the New Testament in word and deed. He was also living out his own special interpretation of New Testament principles that had been forged during those important and formative years in Central America. This is what this volume is all about. Read it and be refreshed!

Hugh Steven
Santa Ana, CA
1984

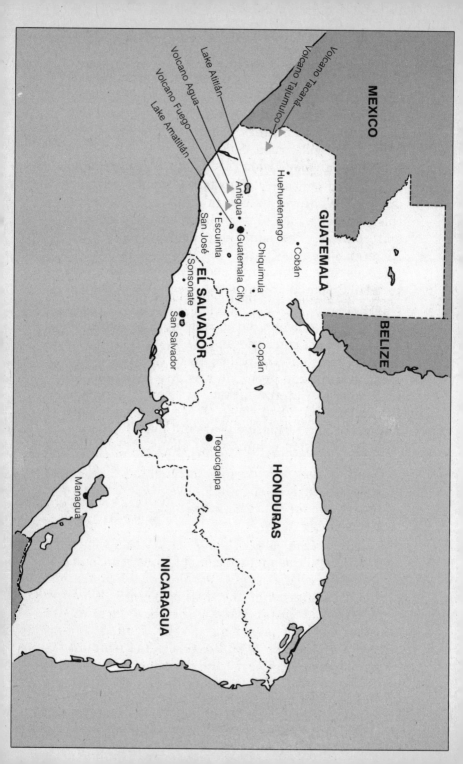

— 1 —

FAR FROM THE MADDING CROWD

Land sold for thirteen dollars per acre in his hometown. You could buy a dozen eggs for twenty-seven cents, a loaf of bread went for nine cents, milk was twenty-two cents a quart, delivered to your door. And you could buy a ready-to-wear man's tailored suit for fifteen dollars.

The word *Sunkist* had just been introduced into the American lexicon as a symbol of quality citrus fruit. Most adults had grown up on farms and in rural communities. Their ideals were romantic, and moral values solid and unchanging. This was reflected in such popular novels as Zane Grey's *Riders of the Purple Sage* and Jean Webster's *Daddy Long Legs*.

There were also strong new social currents stirring in the mainstream of American culture: women's voting rights, prohibition of liquor and the development of the motion picture. Woodrow Wilson had just completed his first term as the twenty-eighth president of the United States, swept into office over Roosevelt and Taft on the assumption that he would not commit Americans to the conflict in Europe. The year was 1917, and William Cameron Townsend was twenty-one.

It was the year that the U.S. government purchased the Virgin Islands from Denmark for
twenty-five million dollars, Russia's Bolshevik
Revolution was just beginning, and Germany
resumed unrestricted submarine warfare. Had he
been interested (there is no indication that he was),
Cameron Townsend could have heard for the first
time in history, jazz music on phonographs.

But Cameron Townsend heard not the razzle-
dazzle of a new musical art form; he heard the
quiet, persistent voice of God. Amidst the clamor
of a country being revolutionized by industrial
development, his career and spiritual interests led
him "far from the madding crowd." Believing that
the man who has riches without understanding and
doing God's will is like the beasts that perish, he
allowed himself to be influenced by those who
might help him understand the "pull" he was
feeling but couldn't articulate.

Until 1917, the "pull" had been in two directions.
When he graduated from southern California's
Compton High School in 1914, Cam had set his
sights on becoming a teacher. But shortly after his
enrollment at Occidental College in Pasadena,
California, he began to feel a tug toward becoming
a preacher.

During his sophomore year, Cam became impressed with the life of J. Hudson Taylor (missionary
to China in 1854), while reading his biography.
From that reading, major mission tenets lodged in
his mind. Many years later when the moment came
for Cam to form his own missionary organization,
the principles of a pioneering faith mission committed to working within the cultural framework of a
given people emerged clearly as God's direct
guidance.

During the same year, two of Cam's school friends, Elbert (Robbie) Robinson, director of the campus YMCA, and classmate Carroll Byram, invited Cam to attend a special missionary outreach meeting sponsored by the student missionary band. The speaker was none other than the distinguished missions statesman John R. Mott.

Professional in appearance, with heavy eyebrows beginning to show flecks of white, John Mott, at fifty-two, had an impressive list of mission-related and civic achievements to his credit. Mott was both charter member and secretary of the international YMCA – then committed to Christian evangelism. A protégé of D.L. Moody and C.T. Studd of the "Cambridge Seven," Mott became the leader and organizer of the influential Student Volunteer Movement. Taking SVM's rallying cry of "the evangelization of the world in this generation," Mott, with a fervent concern to motivate students to commit themselves to overseas mission work, made aggressive appeals to college and university students throughout the United States. It was Mott, who later won a Nobel Peace Prize and was awarded the distinguished Service Medal for his work in World War I, who captured the attention of young Townsend in January, 1917. After the meeting, in a kind of classic understatement, Cam said simply, "I was impressed with how very little I had done to witness for my faith."

Fresh from that influence, Cam and Robbie answered an advertisement from the Bible House of Los Angeles that appealed to the young men's spirit of adventure and growing concern for world evangelism. The ad called for college students who would be willing to spend a year in Central America as colporteurs or Bible salesmen.

Mr. R.D. Smith was the man who received the applications from Cam and Robbie and lost no time in attempting to secure their names on the "dotted line." Both men were amazed to receive, almost by return mail, a request for an interview with Mr. Smith at the Bible House.

When Mr. Smith interviewed the two men, he was particularly pleased that Cam had some knowledge of Spanish, but was not too optimistic about Cam's ability to physically handle the colporteur's job.

"Quite frankly, I'm concerned about your friend's physical qualifications," said Mr. Smith to Robbie. "There will be a great deal of walking and hard mountain trails in Guatemala."

Robbie assured Mr. Smith that even though Cam's college friends called him "Skinny Townsend," he was a lot stronger than he looked. Robbie then proceeded to explain how Cam spent part of each day helping his father work their small farm near the campus, even going into Los Angeles to sell his father's produce.*

Once satisfied that Cam and Robbie qualified for the job, Mr. Smith answered questions and outlined what they would need to get to Guatemala – money. Neither man had the one hundred fifty dollars for the steamboat passage. Wages for Bible salesmen, the two men learned, were a dollar a day. Cam and Robbie would be given a three-month advance toward expenses, but since they were advised against the folly of being without funds on the field, were urged to have in hand as much of their own money as possible before they left.

---

*For a more detailed account of William Cameron Townsend's early life, see the book *Uncle Cam* by James and Marti Hefley, Word Books, 1974.

As the weeks and months passed, money for their boat passage to Guatemala became less and less of a concern. Both men believed they could earn their passage during the summer, working on one of California's many ranches. What did concern Cam and Robbie was the United States April 6 declaration of war on Germany.

Early in his junior year of college, Cam, out of a keen sense of patriotism, had joined the National Guard along with his friend Carroll Byram. Because he held the rank of corporal, Cam felt certain he would be called upon to fight in Europe. Also, Robbie, believing it his patriotic duty to become involved in the war effort, was thinking seriously of joining officer's candidate school.

When the two men presented this new concern to Mr. Smith at the Bible House, he suggested they might apply for a deferment. Then in the same breath, he asked if they would talk with a recently returned missionary from Guatemala. "Her name," said Smith, "is Stella Zimmerman."

More out of courtesy to Mr. Smith, and with a certain amount of curiosity, Cam and Robbie arranged to meet Miss Zimmerman later that week. It was a never-to-be-forgotten experience. Stella Zimmerman, as recorded in Hefley's book, *Uncle Cam*, was a tall, angular blonde about ten years older than Cam who enthusiastically told the men about Guatemala's rich history and beauty and the great need for the people to have the Word of God.

However, when Stella learned that Cam was in the National Guard and that both he and Robbie were considering backing out of their commitment to sell Bibles in Guatemala, she, with white-hot fury said, "You men are cowards! There are a million other men going off to war, yet you two are leaving us women to do the Lord's work alone!"

That encounter with Stella Zimmerman and its eventual outcome is, of course, history. Cam did ask and received deferment. Actually, he displayed his diplomatic prowess early in his life by asking his history professor, Robert McClellan, to write a letter to the captain of Cam's guard unit requesting such a deferment.

That captain's now-classic reply was, "Go. You'll do a lot more good selling Bibles in Central America than you would shooting Germans in France."

Thus on August 18, 1917, William Cameron Townsend and his friend Robbie Robinson, not unlike Homer's "kingly man," stepped into the pages of history.

From *Beowulf* to Homer's *Odyssey* to Tolkien's *Lord of the Rings*, the adventurous "quest" has been a metaphor for a moral journey. It is the vehicle through which a young hero's spiritual and physical qualities are tested. By suffering and trial and by encounters with strange and amazing adventures, he proves his worthiness to rule the kingdom. After each encounter with evil, after every test of temptation and despair, after all the victories in the face of certain defeat, the hero's faith is imperceptibly strengthened. In his growth from innocence to experience, he learns he is stronger at the end of the journey than he was at the beginning. He now has more courage, wisdom insight and strength. More importantly, as he catches certain glimpses of divine purpose behind each event and trial, he has come to the firm conviction that it was, after all, God who was testing him; it was God who had chosen him to carry out His will.

Cam and Robbie were in every way classic heroes as they ventured into unknown and alien territory, far from the warm support of family and friends.

— 2 —

BEGINNING OF THE QUEST

The summer was long, hard and hot. They pulled weeds, planted corn, cut the heads off rye, wheat and oats with a header wagon, and memorized Spanish verbs and Scriptures while they worked the fields of the thousand-acre Smith Ranch in Corcoran, California, fifty miles south of Fresno.

Cam, Robbie, Sig Lindstrum, and two other college students began their ranch work at the end of April, 1917. In a letter home, Cam wrote, "In spite of the long hours, the boss never rushes the fellows. In fact, the old crew is pretty lazy and 'crabs' whenever we work hard. They need a foreman on the ranch and a little system."

The hours may have been long, but there were moments to play a few college pranks. Wrote Cam, "Robbie and I put a horned toad in Sig's bed tonight. He is just going to bed as I write this, so am expecting.... Well it came with a little wrestling match!"

On August 18, a Saturday, Cam and Robbie said good-bye to parents and friends at the old Los Angeles Union train station. Their plan was to travel to San Francisco and secure passage on a

ship bound for Guatemala. It was here they met
their first obstacle – delay!

Well, we're off. Left Los Angeles at five o'clock on
the Santa Fe. Had a wonderful send-off. I've got the
greatest folks God ever blessed a fellow with. I am
excited and happy to at last be on my way, but the
separation from my parents and relatives was hard.
What a special joy to be sent away with a prayer and a
smile from a mother and father who have done so much
for me. All credit to them for giving their son to the
Lord's service in such a distant land. I know it's hard
on them. It is to them that I give thanks to God for
teaching me to honor and obey the Lord.

So many friends met us at Pasadena. It was great to
see them. One dear friend, Mrs. Addeman, fixed us a
lunch. I've broken into it already. It's wonderful to
have friends! May God help me to make more and to be
as true as steel to all of them. *Adelante, siempre adelante!* Eyes to the front, forward march!

Principle of friendship.

Of all the principles Cameron Townsend lived by,
his most basic was to make and be a friend to
people – all people. With Paul, Cam would say,
"Do as I do, and follow my example." Cam wanted
every Wycliffe member to treat people with
courtesy and honor, to entertain others in their
homes and never allow the busyness of "the work"
to override showing hospitality with sincere joy.

On one occasion, a colleague asked Mr. Townsend if perhaps it would be wise to meet a certain
influential man in the hope that he would help the
organization. Said Mr. Townsend, "We do not 'try'
to meet influential people, but if God brings them
across our path or gives us providential encounters
with them, we try to be faithful friends."

The delay Cam and Robbie met was in their ship's sailing date. It was due to sail on September 15. But this was only part of the problem. The war in Europe had greatly reduced West Coast shipping which caused a heavy demand for tourist-class accommodation. When the men inquired about passage, the agent told them the only available space was first class. Since they wanted to go tourist class, they would have to wait six weeks for the next available ship or work for the difference between tourist and first-class fare which was thirty-five dollars each.

August 18, 1917. We worked nights at the Wells Fargo warehouse. They paid $65.00 per month. We stayed two weeks. In order to save as much money as we could for our passage, we lived largely on poached eggs and milk. I had a box of candy that had been given to me at the train station. It stood me in good stead. I must say I certainly don't like Frisco's waterfront.

Thursday, August 30. We quit work and spent three days in Berkeley visiting the Dyke family. It was here our friend Dr. Powell offered to cut out our tonsils free. We had it done on Friday morning. The ether affected Rob pretty badly, but I didn't notice it a bit. The doc said my operation was much worse than Rob's because my tonsils were large and my mouth small. I believe him. My throat sure feels like it! We were two pretty sick fellows.

Thankful to be able to stay at Charlie Dyke's. They took great care of us and made us feel absolutely at home. By Wednesday evening we were able to go back to San Francisco and look for work. But even though we pulled every string imaginable, we couldn't find a single job. I think it was because we still looked pretty weak after our operation. On Friday we decided to go first-class and booked passage through one of Mr. Dyke's friends in Oakland.

We were able to get twenty-five percent off for missionary discount. Going first class must be a provision of the Lord. I don't think our throats were in condition to handle the steerage food. The Lord has guided us wonderfully in all our plans. Our fare will be $84.75 instead of $113.00.

Saturday, September 15. We are off again. Left San Francisco aboard the S.S. *Pacific Mail* at 6:00 and are now (7:45) just passing out of sight of the lights around the Golden Gate. The sea is calm and the ship glides smoothly through the waters that are awash in the golden hue of a setting sun. What a blessed day this has been! We bade farewell to many of our friends at the Dyke's home. Mr. Dyke thought I had too much baggage. Actually, it was mostly Bibles and Scripture portions; I only had one small suitcase. The Dykes can't be beat. They continually open their home to missionaries. On one occasion they had nineteen staying with them!

Mr. Dyke and Sig Lindstrum had a little trouble getting on board with us earlier today, but Sig's army uniform and Mr. Dyke's federal pass got them on. We inspected our cabin and then all went to lunch (the sailing had been postponed until 4:00). It was our first meal on board. How splendid to have Sig and Mr. Dyke as our guests.

Saying good-bye was, as always, hard. I watched them as they waved good-bye and wondered what they will be doing and where they will be when I return. Sig will probably be in France by Christmas.

After watching the Golden Gate, we returned to the dining salon. Since this was the eve of Mexico's independence, the salon was decorated in red, white and green, Mexico's national colors.

There was a festive party going on and in the drinking of healths, Central America was not forgotten! I thought how appropriate it was for Rob and me to be beginning our work on the eve of the celebration of this great Mexican liberator, Father Hidalgo. Here we were, two colporteurs carrying the message of the Great Liberator who said, "If the Son shall set you free, ye shall be free indeed."

Sunday, September 16, Mexican Independence Day. Slept gloriously our first night at sea. We awoke much rested and not a bit seasick. The sea is smooth and the ship heavily laden so that it rolls very little. As a result, few have succumbed [to sea sickness]. Practically everyone on board speaks Spanish. We started in right away to try to improve our knowledge of this beautiful language. There are two young fellows who live in Guatemala City who have the cabin next to ours. One of them, Alberto Aguera, has agreed to teach us Spanish.

We had a dense fog all day today and the ship is only making about eight miles per hour.

> For the next six days Cam and Robbie had little to do but read and study Spanish, make acquaintances and eat.

The meals are great. At our table is a party of five Americans. They have seen a good bit of the world. Most are headed for the mines in Chile.

One of the men is terribly plagued with asthma, yet he thinks nothing of spending most of his working life at fifteen thousand feet above sea level. I think he'll choke up and die within a month, but he is lured on by the hope of making a stake.

Another tough old miner, whose best days were spent in the silver mines of Mexico, had talked a happy-go-lucky fellow into taking a half interest with him in a coconut farm near Manzanillo. The chances are one hundred to one they will lose their whole investment.

Among the Central Americans is a couple that owns a plantation in El Salvador. He is Swiss and went to El Salvador to seek his fortune. His wife is the heiress of a wealthy Salvadoran landowner who had hoped his daughter would marry a wealthy foreigner. His wish was fulfilled and now they have a son-in-law who spends his money lavishly. In San Francisco I saw him tip the dockhands twenty-five dollars in as many minutes. He gave anyone a tip who did him the slightest service. How sad to realize that his generosity was all for show. In all probability (like ninety-nine percent of these planters), he pays his farmhands fifteen to twenty-five cents per day while he throws away the money he made by their sweat.

Principle of treating employees with fairness and consideration.

From the beginning of his ministry, Cameron Townsend championed the cause of human rights long before it became a popular issue in the 70's and 80's. "I always felt it was important, in some way, to show the world the injustice being done to the Indian peoples by landowners and others. This was the reason I wrote my novel, *Tolo*.* I wanted people to be aware of what life was like for Indian peoples in Latin America. I discovered many local employers refused to pay decent wages to their employees. This is wrong. Stinginess is inexcusable; it's a sin. So is anger. Don't be stingy or angry with your employees, pay wages equal to the best in the area." In every way he could, Cameron Townsend honored the dignity of Indian peoples. He was concerned for their well-being and always

---

Tolo, The Volcano's Son, a novel by William Cameron Townsend, Wycliffe Bible Translators, Inc. 1981 (originally *Revelation Magazine*, Philadelphia, 1936).

looked for ways to help them realize their potential.

When the fog cleared after the second day, we ran into a great school of porpoises. One day we saw a whale spouting and some flying fish. The weather is clear and the sun waxes hotter with every league. We spotted large turtles off the coast of lower California.

In all, the trip has been quite pleasant. One of our new friends is a man who has been all over the world. He said on one trip from Australia to London he was out of sight of land for more than five months. I myself would have enjoyed such a trip if all sailing was as great as this.

I started a sermon of my own in Spanish and a translation of one by Dr. Chapman I found in the *Christian Herald*. The inspiration for my sermon came from Spurgeon's sermon on the seasons. Afterward, Alberto corrected it for me. It was a little different reading than what he has been used to!

The sea remains calm and smooth. The ship's doctor says he has never known it to be this way so far south. One fellow thinks someone is praying for calm seas for the sake of someone on board. I might have told him that the Dykes prayed that at best we might be spared from seasickness. I gave out a couple of tracts and a gospel among the waiters.

Principle of never overlooking an opportunity to witness.

A basic premise of Cameron Townsend's life that began early and continued into advanced years was to never overlook an opportunity to give a positive word of witness. He drew a sharp line between personal faith and mere knowledge. He believed all faith rested on authority, and since the highest authority was the Word of God, he tried whenever possible to bring whomever he could into contact

with this Authority. At special banquets or around
the breakfast table, Cam frequently asked a visiting dignitary to read a selected passage of Scripture, and it was a common practice for Cam to give
a copy of the New Testament to the driver of his
cab, or in the case of the incident below, a hotel bell
clerk.

In September, 1976, Mr. Townsend, then age
eighty, took part in a Congress of Americanists in
Paris, France. It was a particularly difficult time
for him and for the work of SIL. The congress,
made up of people who strongly opposed SIL's
involvement with indigenous peoples had, in one
meeting, hooted and stamped their feet in order to
drown out the reading of a paper given by an SIL
staffer.

Dick Hugoniot, then director of SIL's work in
Nepal, had come to inform Mr. Townsend that the
working agreement for SIL to continue in Nepal
had not been renewed and SIL workers were beginning to leave.

"I arrived tired, travel-worn and dirty," said
Dick. "When I told Uncle Cam the news of Nepal,
he asked after the SIL workers, then sensing my
fatigue, gave me the keys to his hotel room and
invited me to take a shower and freshen up. I did.
Later when I came down from his room, I discovered Uncle Cam in warm conversation with the
hotel bell clerk. He was talking to him about the
Lord. I learned later Cam had given him a New
Testament (*Good News for Modern Man* in
French) the day before. Now Cam was interested
to know if the young man had been reading it.

"The bell clerk was a bit skeptical, but out of
respect for an old man, assured Cam that he would
indeed read the book.

"I shall remember that moment for the rest of my life. Uncle Cam was in the middle of a terribly harsh and tension-filled period in his life when he and his organization were being bitterly attacked. He had important meetings to attend, tight schedules to keep plus people to meet, including ambassadors and other highly-placed government officials, and here he was spending time and being concerned for the spiritual well-being of a bell clerk."

We had a great argument on deck this morning. I tried to stick up for President Wilson and defend his statement that we are fighting the German military system – Kaiserism -- and that we have nothing personally against the German people, but the men came down on me thick and fast from all quarters. After that argument, we shifted onto all sorts of discussions. An American rancher from Mazatlán took off on a tirade on the Yellow Peril, Black Peril, labor and capital strifers and most of the ills and aches of the United States. It was good practice for me. I had a mighty hard time passing off my idealistic arguments that I learned in school.

There is a good bit of fast living and gambling on board. One evening some of the steerage passengers and a group of our mining friends went below for a big gambling game. A couple of guitars and an accordion made music – vanity, vanity!

Robbie and I tried our efforts at missionary work. The Latin Americans were polite and listened, but, oh, how we were squelched by the Americans on board. They told us frankly we were fools. I thought about the miner who suffered from asthma who willingly endangered his life in the quest for gold. Such superficial pursuit in comparison to the privilege of serving our Lord and taking the Gospel to the lost! Truly the preaching of the Cross is foolishness to those who are lost.

One evening the American rancher from Mazatlán tried to dissuade me from "wasting my life in trying to convert Mexicans." I think I handled him too softly. Oh for more righteous indignation and the power to express it with such keenness as Christ did !

One evening as we got up from the supper table, we sighted a steamer. It was the first we had seen since leaving San Francisco. Everyone ran up on deck to see it. To my surprise it was running almost without lights, but lighted up when it answered our whistle. It proved to be the S.S. Peru of this line. After supper I played several games of checkers with Alberto.

Friday, September 21. Today we ran very slowly. The captain said that if we went full speed, we would reach Mazatlán along in the afternoon and it would be too late to do anything. He decided to slacken up and not arrive until Saturday morning. I thought yesterday we rounded Cape St. Lucas but it was an island off Magdalena. We went around St. Lucas early this morning and we have been sailing nearly due east across the gulf all day.

The sea is as smooth as glass and the reflections of the clouds in the water are beautiful. We saw a large school of tropical seals close to the ship. There are also a lot of big turtles or tortoises. The larger ones are about a foot and a half across. I was told the best shells are worth $12.00 a pound. The moonlight on the water tonight is beautiful. Mazatlán tomorrow. *Buenas noches.*

— 3 —

GETTING THERE

In 1914, President Woodrow Wilson had ordered American forces to temporarily seize the port of Veracruz in old Mexico. His reason – to prevent the supply of arms by Germany to General Huerta's federal troops. A year earlier, Mexico's President Madero had been imprisoned and ultimately assassinated. Mexico was in the middle of intense political and social upheaval. But by September 1917, when Cam Townsend sailed into Mazatlan's harbor, Mexico was enjoying a period of relative tranquility. The revolts led by Pancho Villa in the north, Emiliano Zapata in the south and Huerta's forces were all but suppressed.

The man most responsible for this stabilization was Venustiano Carranza, the governor of the state of Coahuila. In spite of his patriarchal appearance, Carranza was a tough horseman and fighter who convened a constitutional congress that drew up the basic Mexican constitution that prevails to this day. Thus on February 5, 1917, Carranza became the first of Mexico's presidents to be elected under a legal constitutional process.

Saturday, September 22, 1917. One of the men woke us up at about 6:30 this morning to see the entrance to

Mazatlan's harbor. It's shaped like a horseshoe and I could see two rocky promontories with several small rocky islands around them. On top of the highest island was a lighthouse, said to be the highest in the world. About seven o'clock we pulled into a narrow channel and anchored. An American gunboat that patrols the coast was anchored just in front of us. A little further in was a small Mexican steamer that provided service to the Mexican ports along the coast.

To the south of us is a stranded hulk of a Mexican gunboat that had been destroyed by the revolutionists who in 1913 captured the promontory to the west of the harbor and began shelling the cruiser. The gunboat went in too close to return fire and went aground. It was then at the mercy of the revolutionists who sunk it and killed *muchos hombres*.

After breakfast we boarded a launch and went ashore. The town is spread out along the sandy waterfront and dotted quaintly with coconut palms and the remains of two or three wharves. The last one was washed away by a flood two days before we arrived. Behind the wharves are a big warehouse and government buildings.

Conveyance to the center of town is reached by climbing into a rickety old carriage dragged along by skinny little mules. Rob and I decided to walk and see the sights. The streets are narrow with one-story shops and houses built right up against the sidewalk, snug against one another. The walls are made from sun-dried adobe brick, smoothly plastered and brightly painted (oranges, yellows, blues, purples, reds).

The sidewalks are likewise narrow and made more uncomfortable by iron-barred windows that project a foot or so out from the face of the wall.

The main streets are paved with cobblestones so that when rigs and carts, mules and oxen clatter over them, it makes a hideous racket.

I was most interested in the market. It was held in a large building that occupied all of a square. Around the outside edge of the building on the sidewalks, and even in the gutters, people had set up little stands – drygoods, fruit, bakery goods, drinks – soft and hard, all colors and in bottles of all descriptions. The candy, too, was brightly colored. Rob bought lemonade colored red. I wasn't interested. The *nieve de leche* (snow milk) or ice cream was more tempting.

Inside the building, the market was arranged with some system. Drygoods and novelties were in one section, vegetables in another, meat in another, and so on. The lunch counter occupied an open corridor.

For the remainder of the day, Cam and Robbie visited what Cam called the "more refreshing" sights of the city. These included a gospel mission where a group of Mexican children sang praises to the Savior, a school, hospital and a modern drug store with "showcases and an up-to-date soda fountain." They also visited a Presbyterian church where inside the beautiful church courtyard, Pastor José Flores treated the two men to guavas (Cam noted they were several times larger than the ones he was used to in California). The two men said they hoped they could return for services the following day.

As they continued their inspection of the town, Cam puzzled over how people made a living. "No one seems to have anything to do." This notion was further reinforced when he looked into a small blacksmith shop hidden behind a brick wall and found three men, "with absolutely nothing to do. And if there is some small task to do, it is shared by several people."

I noticed that most of the people go barefooted or else

wear leather sandals. Some of the people are dressed
right up to the latest U.S. style. During the revolution,
most of the foreigners and wealthy Mexicans moved to
the States or Havana. Many are just now commencing to
return.

Before the revolution, the streets were well-main-
tained and brilliantly lighted. They are now poorly
lighted. A year ago it was risky to be on the streets
after seven o'clock. The city is normal now. They say
President Carranza has things pretty well in hand. I am
happy for this; people are tired of unsettled conditions.
However, out among the ranches the bandits are still
quite numerous. Just lately two men were killed and
robbed of their pack train. The trains, however, are still
running to all parts of the country, except when the
bridges are washed out. There is railway service from
here to Nogales, Arizona. It takes four days. There is
is also a four-day service from here to Mexico City.

We visited an old fort. It is vacated now, but an old
cannon remains and the walls are full of bullet holes.
The present town garrison consists of about one thousand men. We watched the review at one of the bar-
racks. There were a few white uniforms and a few had
guns, but most were without guns and had overall suits
or old clothes for their uniforms. Many had sandals
instead of shoes. A few had leggings. The epaulets are
sewed onto the shirt unless the officer is fortunate (or
unfortunate – it's awfully hot) to have a coat. I went up
to one fellow who had a lot of braids and tassels on his
sleeves, stood at attention and saluted. He straightened
up and returned the salute. I then asked him the name
of his general. He said, "Carrasco."

We visited the jail where we saw a number of prison-
ers taking things easy in the cells. There seemed to be
a trial going on in the courtroom, but we weren't able to
distinguish between the judge, the lawyers and the

prisoner. The city hall is some distance away on one side of the cathedral plaza. It has a very pretty patio. One of the police lieutenants wanted me to wait and visit his chief, but it was time to catch the launch back to the ship. However, I already had quite a visit with the lieutenant.

I learned the municipality owns the water system which is very good. The water is piped in from a distance of 125 miles. The library is small but free to all. They also have a free hospital that Rob says is very good. He went through it while I visited the municipal building. They perform quite serious surgical operations.

The cathedral, like the municipal building, faces the main plaza. It is a grand old building with two tall bell towers in front and a large dome in the rear. There are two tall columns outside the door and about a dozen columns of some beautiful stone, line the main aisle. There are images all around that old women worship with the most abject hungering look I ever saw. There is a cross by the door that people kiss and then lick the base which is black as a result. There are several other cathedrals. The people who attend seem to be nearly all women and children. At the Presbyterian church, on the other hand, there were eighteen men in the Bible class and more came to the preaching service.

There are a few fine establishments but I saw only one large show window. I was surprised to find a good many sewing machines in the homes. Most were old-time Singers. Despite the sewing machines, most of the little kids were clad in naught but robes of sunshine. Others wore little shirts too small to button. They were cool, which is more than I could say of myself!

Sunday we had to pay $1.10 roundtrip to go ashore. I went to church, but Rob had received an eleven o'clock invitation to an American-Mexican home. He had met the father, who is a son of the American consul, the evening before. The mother was Mexican and he said that the daughters were charming. He must have made a hit for when he came away, he found two stamp pictures in his hat band. Rob says he had a great time. Church service was fine. I met a Japanese man from Seattle who spoke good English. He seemed pleased to meet an American. We got back to the ship late and had to eat a cold lunch. We sailed shortly after four o'clock.

Monday, September 24. It's not quite as hot this morning. A considerable breeze is blowing, but it's bad enough. I read and wrote most of the day but was too lazy to accomplish much. We sighted some large fish which have jaw-like fins with which they hold a person while they suck his blood. This afternoon I had a fine talk with a young importer from Guadalajara, Mexico. He told me about the industries of the Pacific slope. He's interested in purebred cattle.

Just before suppertime Rob got into quite an argument about the Bible and Christianity. I waded in, too. It did us good to confirm our faith, but it made us sad to find there were so few, if any, professing Christians on board. About eight o'clock a hard rain came up. I wouldn't have been surprised to see a storm, but it didn't come. (Lost my knife overboard doing acrobatic stunts – the one Papa gave me.)

Tuesday, September 25. We arrived in Manzanillo harbor at six this morning, two days after leaving Mazatlán. It has a prettier setting and a better harbor than Mazatlán. It's deep right up to the shore. There is a breakwater and there used to be a pier where vessels could dock, but it was burned in the revolution. A Mexican warship was tied up to its remains. We went ashore right after breakfast. It cost us fifty cents roundtrip apiece. I took a picture of the stevedores unloading a barge and then looked over the town. It is a mere village compared to Mazatlán, although much more picturesque. The harbor is surrounded by hills through which there are two gaps to the lake which lies just back of the hills. The main street runs through one gap. The other was cut through for the railroad that runs out across the lake to Colima, Guadalajara, and Mexico City.

The houses are most all built of wood; a few are made of brick. Two or three along the lake were of palm leaves. In fact, the lake town looked for all the world like pictures I have seen of African villages. As we walked back to the lake, we passed a school that was in session. Everything looked modern and attractive and I went in to visit while Rob went to the lake. The teacher was a little embarrassed but was glad to have me. She had the children recite and sing and show off what they had learned. It was the first grade and they did very well. There are four grades and two teachers. They were all girls. The boys attend another school.

After that I found Rob and we went down to the lake. A festival seemed to be going on and we stopped to inquire. It proved to be a double wedding. The music and dancing were going on under a palm-covered arbor. The bakery, a short distance away, was busy preparing pastry for the feast. It seemed the whole town was there to celebrate. We didn't attend, but went around to where three little *muchachos* [children] were bathing in the lake. They posed for a penny apiece while Rob took their picture. Despite the poverty of the town, many of the homes had their Singer sewing machines. We visited the brick cathedral, but it consisted mostly of a large bell dated 1882 and a beautiful cool patio high up on the hill overlooking the harbor. The American consul had a home and tennis court even higher up.

We went back to the station and found Antonio

Martín del Campo, the importer who suggested a walk
to the bathing beach. He pointed out a cross painted on
the cliff by the trail which he said always meant that
someone had died there. At the beach he treated us to a
coconut apiece. They cut both ends of the thick green
pod with a machete. One serves as the bottom of the
cup and the top is cut clear through the inner shell to
the coconut water which is drunk. After that they cut
the fruit in two and then eat the white meat. This was
the first time either of us had ever eaten fresh coconut.
After bidding good-bye to the Campo brothers and
buying a newspaper, we went around rocks and had a
swim. Rob had his B.V.D.'s and we took turns using
them. It was most refreshing. We then came aboard.
The steamer sailed at five o'clock. Good-bye Mexico!

For the next four days, the *Pacific Mail* sailed
across the Gulf of Tehuantepec, through rough,
choppy water, rain, spectacular thunder and lightning, and gale winds that at one point reduced the
steamer's speed to six knots an hour.

Through it all, Cam recorded the events in simple
unfettered prose. "My stomach isn't right today.
Not enough exercise." To pass the remainder of the
time aboard ship, Cam wrote an accurate account
of Mexico's agriculture, mining and lumbering
products, listing them state by state. He commented about the terrible devastation caused by
the revolution and noted with sadness that one of
Mexico's ills was a lack of advancement opportunities available for the average person – the peons.
He expressed hope that soon Mexico would recover
from her economic problems and be on the road to
prosperity.

On Saturday, September 29, Cam wrote that he
had at last sighted the land of their destination. He
knew this was Guatemala because he saw a large

number of beautiful volcanoes from the deck of the
ship. On that day Cam said he woke early and before breakfast read twenty-one chapters of the
Book of Job, then completed the remaining twenty-
one chapters after breakfast. He wrote that it took
him from December 4 to September 29 inclusive to
read through the entire Bible. He then noted it was
his plan to spend the next several months reading
his New Testament in Spanish, with a passing
remark that some portions of the Old Testament in
Spanish were "pretty hard."

About noon we passed the first port of Guatemala —
Ocós. It's about twenty or thirty miles from Champerico, our first stop. We arrived at Champerico about
four o'clock and dropped anchor about a mile from
shore in six and a half fathoms of water. We didn't
venture too close here. There is nothing but a beach and
the land swells roll the vessel about badly. Seven or
eight years ago, a German freighter was driven ashore
at Ocós. It was just salvaged a few months ago. Although there is a railroad and telegraph terminus at
Champerico, the town doesn't amount to much. Just a
few buildings and a pier in sight. The surrounding country seems to be covered with forests of some kind. We
sent a telegram to Mr. Edward Bishop, Field Director
of the Central American Mission. Ten words cost thirty-
five cents! They have unloaded a lighter [flat-bottomed
barge] of lead onto the ship already. There must be a
mine back in the mountains. We are packing up ready
to leave early Monday morning. Hurray!

Sunday, September 30. It stormed badly last night.
The thunder and lightning were terrific. This morning
they didn't commence unloading until eight o'clock and
after that the stevedores continued to take their time.
They have about six lighters. The steam launch hauls a
lighter alongside and when it is full, the launch hauls it

to the pier where it is unloaded. It's a slow process. It looked like rain this evening so they didn't bring out any more lighters for fear the flour would get wet. Consequently we had to lay over for one and a half lighters of freight. The captain said it would cost the company one thousand dollars.

It didn't rain after all. We won't reach Guatemala City now until Tuesday. I will be glad to get off. This lazy life doesn't agree with me. I only weigh 131½ pounds. [He was five feet, ten inches tall.] Besides, sleeping at anchor at these beach ports isn't as pleasant as it might be. The hot, tropical sun increases the discomfort and impatience of the passengers. One can stick in bed when he's asleep, but when awake he needs to brace himself with pillows or roll out for sure, as the ship rolls badly in the choppy waves. Robbie and I are indeed being introduced to a land where we are being forced to lean hard upon the promise of Isaiah 40:31, "They shall *walk* and not faint."

Monday, October 1, San José de Guatemala. The men and lighters were really at work by seven o'clock this morning, and we said good-bye to Champerico shortly after nine. I spent about half an hour trying to type on the wireless operator's typewriter before sailing. The chief operator is from Santa Ana, California. I used my eyes very little today as they are quite inflamed. The glare from the water is bad on them. We arrived at San José at 5:30, but won't leave the boat until tomorrow morning. It is hard to realize we have arrived.

Tuesday, October 2. We were up bright and early this morning and ready to disembark by six o'clock. The lighter pulled alongside about seven o'clock. They loaded our luggage first, then brought out the chair. It was a box with a seat at each end for two, and ropes on which to attach the pulley of the derrick, or whatever they call it. Robbie and I, plus two other passengers, climbed in first, the power was thrown on and we sailed up into the air a bit, out over the deck and then down into the lighter. Six more were swung over and then we were tossed about on the waves until the steam launch came out and towed us into the iron pier. We were then lifted up in an iron cage and landed on Guatemala soil. After the customs officials had received liberal tips, we ran to the train station, purchased our tickets and soon we were on our way to the metropolis of Central America – Guatemala City.

— 4 —

IT'S GREAT TO BE
"IN THE WAY"

Roughly the same size as Tennessee, the Central American Republic of Guatemala shares its northern border with Mexico; Honduras flanks its eastern frontier and the Pacific Ocean and El Salvador lies to the south. Almost two-thirds of this republic is covered by the mighty Sierra Madre mountains and its smaller chains. And sprinkled throughout are more than two dozen volcanoes, many still active.

More than half of Guatemala's population are descendants of the vast complex Mayan civilization. Ruins of their once-great palaces, temples and city-states that flourished more than 1,500 years ago, lie on the country's eastern plains.

Cam had yet to discover the grandeur of Guatemala's snowcapped volcanoes, green jungle valleys, sparkling blue lakes and its ethnic people who dressed as colorfully as nature had dressed the countryside. His major concern that October 2nd morning, was to secure enough local currency for the trip to Guatemala City.

Five of their traveling companions were taking a special coach on the train, but since they had insufficient funds, Cam, Robbie and two other companions had to part company with their wealthier friends and travel second class.

The train runs on a narrow-gauge track and makes fairly good time. Stations are quite numerous. I noticed the forests have been exploited near the coastal stations. There were many carloads of dye woods, mahogany and Spanish cedar.

We passed a number of cattleherds and villages that consisted mostly of thatched houses, nearly hidden by thick jungle growth. Every settlement had a squad of barefoot soldiers in tattered uniforms standing guard.

At 11:45 we arrived at Escuintla. It's an active little city, quite different from San José that had just a few two-story dilapidated wooden buildings and a swamp in the middle of town ringed with a few thatched huts. Here the train stopped three hours for dinner.

Our traveling companions, Mr. Asturias and Raul, went with Rob and me to find the famous baths, but we couldn't find a carriage, so our companions backed out. They went to a local hotel for lunch. Upon the recommendation of some other friends, Rob and I went to a hotel run by an American named Gilbert. The meal was well-cooked, and by way of luxury, we had ants on the table! The waiter walked about silently. He wore no shoes and the floor was hard-packed earth. Our appetites were ravenous and we enjoyed the food. They say it's the best eating place in Central America.

After eats we visited the cathedral and a boy took me up into the bell tower and up onto the roof from whence I took a picture. One of the bells bore the date 1802. We then listened a little to a band that seems to play in the plaza at all hours. Next we went through an industrial school. On our way back to the tram station, a hard rain shower came up. The train was late so we waited in the railway superintendent's office. The superintendent was an American named Mr. Gleason who had attended the University of Indiana and Washington. He looked like a veritable soldier of fortune. He came with us to Guatemala City and we became quite chummy.

From the town of Escuintla we began a steep climb. The air was cooler and became more so as the train climbed the foothills. At 3,000 feet we skirted the foot of the famous Agua volcano. (This volcano has a nearby twin called Fuego.)

Just before sunset, we reached the famous Lake Amatitlan. It was a beautiful sight with volanoes on either side and a brim of hills all round. The quaint town of Amatitlan stood at the edge of the lake and was reflected in its clear blue waters. The sky's deeper blue was set off by an edging of pure white clouds. The track skirted in and out along the shore and then at its narrowest point crossed right over, dividing the lake in two.

As the sun disappeared, the train climbed to 5,000 feet and into Guatemala City. Rob and I were glad to have overcoats.

It was dark when the train pulled into the station. Stella Zimmerman of the Central American Mission and the assistant pastor of the Cinco Calles [Five Streets] Church were there to meet us. The assistant pastor's name was *Don* José and it was he who guided us to our rooms at the mission. They were neat little rooms in the attic from where we could see the lights of the whole city.

After getting settled, we sat down to a wonderful meal of meat and potatoes and bread to which we did full justice. After supper we just felt fine. Hallelujah, hallelujah, hallelujah! It's great to be in the Way! Now for a year perfectly consecrated to Him. Lord, grant it!

Cam and Robbie spent the next days getting

settled. They began to learn about the culture of their adopted land, practiced their Spanish and learned what was expected of them as newly-appointed Bible salesmen.

Always enthusiastic about food, Cam noted his first meal was a real Guatemalan *desayuno* (breakfast) of bread, cocoa and fruit. Said Cam, "It was good, but not enough."

After his scant breakfast, his first duty was to retrieve his luggage from the train station. It was here Cam began to learn firsthand what it meant for people to be disadvantaged.

Wednesday, October 3, 1917. After breakfast we went to the train station with *Don* José to get our trunk and cases. *Don* José let an Indian carry the trunk and one case. It weighed two hundred pounds and the Indian scarcely weighed one hundred. I would much rather have carried part of it, but was told that it was against the custom here for me to do this.

In the afternoon, Mr. Bishop came and we talked business. Upon his advice, we decided not to get pack mules but to walk and let the Indian worker carry the pack; the pack was not to exceed one hundred pounds. It sounds cruel to me, but Mr. Bishop said that would be the best way to do it. He wants us to stay here in the city until the conference at Antigua* on the 18th. He then would like one of us to stay in Antigua and the other to work among the Indians at Tecpan. Rob is looking forward to giving his life to Indian work, so he will probably go to Tecpan.

Mr. Bishop made arrangements with the cook, *Doña* Elena, to prepare our meals. At first she didn't want to

---

*Once called Antigua Guatemala, this, the second largest city in Guatemala, served as the capital during colonial days. Its name has been shortened to simply Antigua.

because she was afraid we would want American dishes. When we told her to take off the tablecloth and serve up native dishes, she agreed to cook for us. We are to furnish the bread, fruit, salt, sugar, etc. After supper we went to a Bible study in the hall. *Don* José had a fine meeting with a good number present. It's quite cool and rains considerably.

The Central American Mission [CAM] and the Presbyterian Mission have divided the city between them. Each is doing excellent work. CAM has a fine chapel at Las Cinco Calles where as many as seven hundred to one thousand can hear the gospel at once. Not far away they have an orphanage and school. The Presbyterian church has a printing plant, a mission home near the main plaza, and a hospital and girl's school occupy a beautiful site on the north side of town.

Thursday, October 4. This morning we fixed the hall for the examinations of the school children. The school arrived in a body and upon arrival of the examiners, the grill began. The students were quizzed in all their subjects and recited by heart, page after page of material. We listened for a while and were amazed at how little we knew. As I left, I was thankful we didn't have to have our lessons back home word for word.

Later we studied and hiked and saw the sights of the city. When we returned, we helped a missionary family of three – the Aberles from Philadelphia – pack. They were on their way to Honduras.

After supper of another great meal, we went to services and then to bed. Our meals for the day cost only nineteen pesos, or about twenty-five cents apiece.

Friday, October 5. After a splendid Bible study, we spent the day hiking and reading. Before lunch we went to the cemetery, then around the city. The city is well worth seeing. It's built mostly of adobe, though there are some modern buildings made of brick and concrete. Some of the walls are five-feet thick and appear to be absolutely impregnable to earthquakes (of which there are a lot here in Central America).

The sidewalks and pavements are better here than they were in Mazatlán. There are little cars pulled by mules that carry you to all parts of the city. The telephones, banks, and electric lights are all modern-looking. Rob and I were a little disappointed that they were so modern-looking – we wanted them to be more rustic. However, we do get this feeling when we see the oxcarts and barefooted Indian women with bright, distinctive colored costumes. It is plain to see that there are two distinct classes of people here – the thousands of poor and illiterate people who live their lives day by day seemingly without a chance for education or a better life, and the well-educated and wealthy people. I noticed also that vice is rife. Saloons outnumber the stores, and there are plenty of these. Even many of the homes offer something to sell.

In the afternoon we attended a teacher's Bible study conducted by Mr. Bishop. Rob and I were pleased that we understood practically every word. It was one of the best messages I ever heard. There were two points particularly forceful to me:

1. If we judge ourselves, we escape the disciplining chastisement of our Heavenly Father (I Corinthians 11:31).
2. We must meditate on Scripture as well as read it.

Cam concluded his diary that day by saying that while the eats were plain, they were "great." Great, perhaps, because instead of costing them nineteen pesos as they had the day before, their cost was only 18.50 pesos.

The following day Cam was particularly excited

to be invited to Miss Zimmerman's home who, in exchange for Cam and Rob cutting down some tree limbs for firewood, prepared them a regular American dinner, complete with "spuds" to remind them of home.

We made short work of cutting the tree limbs. We wanted to insure another invite! The mail that should have arrived Thursday, hasn't come yet. Haven't heard a word from home since I left. Poor me!

Principle of working together regardless of denominational affiliation.

While Cam and Robbie were still aboard ship, a Guatemalan asked Cam if he was an *evangélico*.* Cam said no believing if he answered yes the young man would think he was connected to some strange cult. He then explained he was Presbyterian and that his friend Robbie was Baptist.

It came as a great surprise for me to learn that evangelical Christians here are called *evangelicos*. I thought how beautiful it would be to have denominational barriers broken down and be closely linked in name, faith, and sufferings with those who believe on the Lord Jesus Christ, and with all who preach His infallible Word. I believe everyone who is guided by the Spirit of God should cultivate the spirit of unity in the bond of love with all who do mission work.

Sunday, October 7. I attended Sunday School at the Presbyterian Mission. They have a splendidly-equipped plant – church building, parsonage, printing press, hospital, and girl's school. About two hundred fifty present at Sunday School, a third of whom were men. More men than women! It's hard for women to leave home to

---

*Spanish for evangelical Protestant.

attend Protestant services. Interestingly, few men are
seen at the Catholic churches. I didn't stay for the
10:45 English service. The Central American Mission
holds Sunday School and preaching in the afternoon,
1:00 to 3:00. Of course Rob and I both attended. Both
meetings were splendid and we could understand it all.
We are progressing rapidly with our Spanish. The
mail, or part of it, came today, but none from home.
Mail for the States leaves Tuesday. If I don't hear
tomorrow, I'll have to write without hearing. We had
another splendid meeting tonight.

Omitted from Cam's journal marking his first
Sunday in Guatemala are two interesting facts.
First, Mr. William Allison, head of the Presbyter-
ian Mission in Guatemala, had invited Cam and
Robbie home for a special Sunday noon dinner.
Joining the two bachelors was Mr. Allison's secre-
tary, a twenty-five-year-old Swedish blonde from
Chicago, Illinois, a Miss Elvira Malmstrom.

After dinner, Elvira entertained the dinner party
with appropriate gospel songs. Bedazzled by
Elvira's voice and the reddish tinge to her blonde
hair, Robbie fell instantly in love. Cam was not at
all impressed.

The second fact had to do with their being late
for Edward Bishop's church service. Lingering
over dinner and listening to Elvira's singing
caused the two men to walk into the service after it
had commenced. Edward Bishop, a no-nonsense
absolutist, said, when Cam and Robbie apologized
for being late, "Don't let it happen again!" Cam
and Robbie flinched.

The date for Cam's departure to Antigua had
been set for October 17. While both men were
anxious to be about the work for which they had

come, they were determined to make the most of their remaining ten days in Guatemala City.

There was, however, one small dilemma that Cam wanted to overcome before he left. He wanted a detailed map of the area he was to work in, but was unable to find anything in any of the bookstores. After appealing to one of the engineers at the railway station, the engineer said he would see what he could find.

Cam's diary reveals they were receiving numerous invitations for lunches and dinners. These came from the Bishops, Stella Zimmerman, and others. With a kind of enraptured bemusement, Cam never failed to express his gratefulness for any meal that had been prepared for him. He did love to eat!

Besides recording who had invited them to dinner, Cam wrote with the eager freshness of his youth about all the new things he was experiencing. About not walking too close to the curb for fear of being struck by the galloping mules propelling the mule-drawn streetcars. He also advised about not being hit by the streetcar itself, and how to board one. "The best way to board the car and not get hit is to jump on as the streetcar dashes by. A roundtrip on one of these streetcars costs five and a half cents."

Friday, October 12. We awoke this morning to the sound of booming cannons. I thought someone was blasting stumps but it proved to be one of the old cannons on the hill behind us replying to a salute from across the valley. About noon I walked to the plaza and found it decorated with flowers and flags. I asked one of the soldiers what it all meant but he didn't know and said it must be a fiesta day. When we found the stores closed in the afternoon, we became real curious and were told it was Columbus Day. This afternoon we had another fine Bible study by Mr. Bishop.

After the meeting, Mrs. Wistar, the widow of the missionary doctor who died last spring, told me some interesting tales of their adventures a few years ago.

One Good Friday in a little town near here, the Catholics had a procession. They stopped in front of the Wistar home and called for them to come out and worship Christ. The part of the procession carrying the image of Christ is always composed of men and there were about two or three hundred in front of the house. They kept calling that Christ was out in the street and if they were really Christians, they should come out and worship Him. Finally, Dr. Wistar went out to speak to them, but he couldn't speak Spanish very well and the people wouldn't listen to him. Instead they began to threaten his life. Mrs. Wistar, who is a cultured Guatemalan, was frightened and stayed inside praying. When she heard the threats to kill her husband, she rushed out to the kitchen and asked the servant girl what she should do. The girl said she wasn't afraid and would go out and speak to the people.

Fearlessly, the servant went out and preached a regular gospel sermon to them. When a man came at her threateningly, she told him to come on, that he couldn't kill her, that Christ had said not to fear those who couldn't kill the soul. He backed away and said he wasn't going to hurt her. Then she went after them for hating the Protestants or *evangélicos*, and said that if they were Christians, they should do as Christ said and love their enemies. Mrs. Wistar said the Lord placed verses from all over the Bible at the girl's command and gave her beautiful diction and keen logic, although only a servant girl. The people saw they were losing ground and the procession moved on.

One by one the days passed, and while Cam faithfully recorded the activities of each day, his diary revealed a growing preoccupation and concern over not receiving a letter from home. Yet characteristically, he made a little joke out of his disappointment.

Sunday, October 14. One month and no word from home! This is very similar to what Sherman called war ....

On the eve of his departure for Antigua and still no word from home, Cam wrote the following letter to his parents.

Guatemala City
October 16, 1917

Dear Home Folks,

The railroad between here and the Atlantic port of Puerto Barrios has been out of commission for a week now. We have had unusually heavy rains for over a week. Consequently, the mails have been disrupted. I doubt if my last week's letter has gotten out of the country. The mail from the States arrived last Saturday, but I received nothing. I am hoping that the delayed mail will arrive today and I will hear from you before I leave for Antigua.

We have been enjoying ourselves immensely. We both are in good health. I had a good bit of constipation last summer and on the boat. I always hike for the toilet just as soon as I get up, whether I want to or not, and I have no trouble at all anymore. I've got the habit! They say that all you need to do down here to get along all right is to keep your bowels open and your mouth shut.

If they had good roads and a water system, Guatemala City would be a health resort. We like it fine. Rob may not return to college next year. He has become very interested in the Indians here and is thinking of making them his life work. He has had a good bit of experience with Indians and likes the high mountains where they live. Besides, they present possibly the most needy field. Considering his age, I believe he will be doing right to stay.

I am still hoping that a way will open for me to return through Mexico. Every map I see I think of a possible route. However, I don't let that take my mind off my work. We will be doing real colporteur work next Monday, at least I will be. Rob will probably be on his way to Tecpan. We will not return to Guatemala City until about November 25 when the missions conference will start and last over Thanksgiving.

Mr. Bishop has loaned us his cots and I have bought another blanket, so we are well fixed for beds. I will have a room at the mission in Antigua where I will stay most of the time. It is thickly populated around Antigua so there will be few trips over a day in length.

We are well equipped. Not using horses during the dry season has made a little difference, but we are well satisfied with our purchases. Living is cheap if you don't buy anything that has been shipped in, i.e., butter or cheese. I sure would like to see an up-to-date *Tribune* and above all get a newsy letter from you folks.

How is the shop, Sunday meetings and everybody? Papa, are you handling any fruit this fall? Apples are fifteen cents a pound down here. Unless one sends a couple of tons or more, parcel post is cheaper than freight and things imported are high. I am sending my diary again for news.

Lazy, but lovingly,
Cameron

— 5 —

DO YOU KNOW MR. JESUS?

Cam and Robbie had carried with them some of the Scriptures they would use, but not all. Several days before Cam left for Antigua, he and Mr. Bishop went to the customs house to pick up a large shipment of tracts and Scriptures he would use as a colporteur. It was one of Cam's first introductions to Latin American government business practices. He would, of course, in the years ahead, become a master diplomat.

The administrator of the customs was a warm, amiable man who said he would have liked to let all two thousand, six hundred pounds of literature go through duty-free. But since he had charged the Catholics duty on their catechisms, he thought it only fair to treat the *evangélicos* the same and charge them duty. Said Cam, "After a good deal of red tape, we finally got our boxes out."

After Cam and Robbie had sorted out and packed the tracts and New Testaments, they were ready to leave for their appointed cities. For his first trip, Cam was to take four thousand tracts. These were to be distributed free of charge. There was, however, to be a charge of three pesos or 7½ cents for the New Testaments. The exception to the rule was that if he found someone who was truly interested in the gospel, but too poor to pay, he could give them a copy.

"The reason we charge," said Mr. Bishop, "is to help the people appreciate the New Testament. They will value it more if they have to pay for it. Otherwise if we just give everyone a copy, the people take them and give them to the priests."

Cam was packed and ready for his trip to Antigua. However, he still didn't have the one thing he felt was necessary for him to be a successful colporteur – a map. Then God worked one of His little miracles Cam had written about earlier.

October 16, 1917. The Indian carrier came early this morning and took most of our tracts. We will take what luggage we have left on the stage. I spent most of the morning trying to find a map, but without success. This afternoon, however, Mr. Austin of the Babson Institute, brought me one. It is a dandy – showing towns, rivers, crops and altitudes. We have to meet two new missionaries (one is a national worker) tonight. Mr. Aberle and I ordered two mattresses for them. Mailed six cards and a letter. Mr. and Mrs. Aberle brought us a big box of home-made candy, and included a one-hundred dollar bill apiece. They sure are a great couple! They said the Lord had given it to them and they would pass it on to us. It is nearly nine o'clock and the missionaries haven't come yet. I hope we don't have another all-night wait.

Wednesday, October 17. The new missionaries arrived at 10:30 last night, but Rob didn't get in until midnight as he took them to a hotel. *Doña* Elena had our breakfast ready by 6:30 and we were down on the sidewalk waiting for the stage by seven o'clock. When the stage arrived, it was full and the driver refused to take us.

The stable manager had promised us passage, so we phoned him. About eight o'clock he sent around a classy rubber-tired taxi cab with an American manager to take us out to Ciudad de Estrada Cabrera where he had phoned to hold the stage. It was the classiest carriage I have ever ridden in. The roads were awful, but we managed to get through. The stage driver, however, had refused to wait for us and they had to phone back for another stage. Our special four-mule stage arrived shortly after nine and we were soon sloshing through the mud and bouncing over the rocks toward Antigua.

The recent torrential rains had caused severe landslides and interrupted the normal flow of traffic, particularly along the north coast. The road to Antigua, a distance of twenty-five miles, was in terrible shape; the first stretch was barely passable. All along the roadside oxcarts were stalled and I marveled that we didn't meet the same fate.

Also sharing the road with the oxcarts and the mule-drawn stage were heavily-burdened Indians. I asked where they had come from and was told that many had walked a distance of thirty miles or more. The men carried weights of over one hundred pounds resting on their backs, held firm by a strap running over the forehead. I had seen Indians in the city carrying over two hundred pounds (my trunk), but not for long distances. The women, too, were burdened. Some carried their produce in baskets; others carried their produce in sheets thrown over their shoulders. Many were further burdened down with their nursing babies. Even children trotted along under burdens. Everyone carried a load.

It is apparent the Indian is Guatemala's beast of burden. I was deeply saddened to see this and vowed to be more faithful than ever in telling those poor people about Him who said, "Come unto me, all ye that labor and are heavy-laden.''

Our first stop was Mixco, a quaint old town set upon the side of a hill. I bought twenty tortillas for a peso – about 2½ American cents. To make the new pastry slide down more easily, and to add a little spice to the diet, I now and then took a piece of the delicious home-made candy Mr. Aberle had given me before I left.

The road from Mixco on was a stiff climb. The four mules were hard put to make it up the steep grade. The roads were rough and the springs in the stage stiff. Rob and I considered it a privilege to get out every once in a while and walk.

About 1:30 we had our last sight of Guatemala City. From our favored position, we could look out over the canyon and see a beautiful view of the city and plateau on which Guatemala City is situated.

After we made the grade and traveled a few miles on level ground, we came to the descent into Antigua. Everyone on the stage talked about how steep it was and how much they dreaded going down. Our driver had already overtaken and passed the six-mule stage that had left two hours ahead of us. Eager to arrive ahead of all the rest, he lashed his mules into a gallop on the downgrade. The seemingly springless old stage creaked, bounced and rolled over the bumps and around the bends. The coachman drove his mules so fast that the collars were often pushed up on the heads of the galloping mules. But even then the driver wasn't satisfied. He leaned out over them so far it seemed to me he would surely fall, and from that position screeched out threats and vulgarities and lashed the mules unmercifully.

When we arrived at the Antigua mission about 3:30 (the other stage arrived at 4:30), we were two bone-weary young men. Mr. Bishop had arrived the day before and was there to give us a warm welcome. After a good supper and a meeting at seven, we wearily retired to our army cots hoping for a long restful sleep. But it wasn't to be. Toward early morning, my scant bedcovers failed to protect me from the cold. Thus Rob and I were up and outside walking to explore the city by five o'clock.

Thursday, October 18. Antigua is surrounded by beautiful green hills. The one exception is to the southwest. Here the fertile valley is covered with coffee plantations that bump right up to the base of the volcano Agua whose conical peak majestically pierces the sky not more than three or four miles away. And there is more. The volcanoes Fuego and Acatenango are also so close that I stood in awe.

Antigua streets are quiet and restful. The city is rightly called Antigua because of its many fine old cathedrals and monasteries. Antigua was once the third capital of Guatemala. The Indian monarch's seat of power had been situated near Tecpan. When Pedro Alvarado, the Spanish captain, destroyed this stronghold, he built a new capital at Ciudad Veija, three miles from where Antigua now stands. Here he left his wife Isabela in charge of his new kingdom while he made an expedition to Peru. During his absence, old Agua erupted and threw out water, mud and boulders upon the capital, destroying it and killing Isabela and many others. The government headquarters was moved to Antigua where it stayed until the city was destroyed by earthquakes in July, 1773.

Up until that time, Antigua had been lively, light-hearted and one of the largest cities of the new world. Her merchants traded with distant markets and her society was most aristocratic. Most of the Roman Catholic religious orders had monasteries within the city. There were ruins of some forty great ecclesiastical orders. To inspect one of them, Rob and I climbed over the stone wall of a coffee plantation. This monastery had a luxurious temple and extensive gardens and living quarters that sheltered fully one thousand monks. The structure was massive, with high arched ceilings and domes that served to awe the worshipers. The old cathedral had been a tremendous building of three long aisles arched over with ceilings of perhaps forty feet high. Each dome bore the coat of arms of some ancient house or order. Some were well-preserved, but most were caved in.

Off the main aisle were smaller chapels of nearly the same height. One of these was used as a burial place for bishops and other dignitaries. Some of their bones outlasted the mortar that enclosed them and were lying around on the floor. Everywhere there is dirt and debris where velvet-clad nobles and silk-gowned ladies formerly worshiped. There was even a razorback sow that someone had tied to the base of a gigantic column.

Before doing any more exploring, Rob and I returned to the mission for breakfast. It was served at seven o'clock and consisted of weak coffee and rolls. They gave us Americans a little hash, but it is not customary. If it were milk instead of coffee I could get along fine, but as it is, I have to eat a lot of rolls to get full. I suppose I will get accustomed to it.

At 8:30 we had our prayer groups and at nine o'clock the first meeting of the conference. Mr. Bishop conducted the Bible study for one hour and thirty minutes. was much deeper than most of what we get in the States. Even the Indians who had flocked in seemed to understand. After the meeting, Rob and I struck out in search of more ruins.

Every block seemed to have massive walls of some old church or monastery. We kept on until we happened upon the largest ruins in the city – those of the San

Franciscan Church and Monastery, which, while similar
to what we had seen earlier, were far more extensive
and covered two or three acres. The sexton opened the
church and showed us through. The belfry was badly
cracked (from the terrible earthquake in 1790), but
there was still one large beautifully tuned bell and
several smaller ones. The large bell bore the date 1754.

The bells also bore engravings that told who had con-
tributed them to the monastery and when. The right
wing of the church had been restored and was used for
worship. There were many ancient paintings and a
small antique pipe organ with a single keyboard that
was being used in the worship.

There were several altars where many indulgences
were offered to all who worshiped there. The images
were numerous and the tips of their toes were black
with the kisses of the thousands of worshipers. It is
here that the Indians come to worship the spirit of the
volcano Agua.

On one side of the wall was the tomb of Hermano
Pedro Betancourt, the outstanding saint of Guatemalan
history. He was the revered founder of the local hospital. It is said he performed miraculous deeds during its
construction. One story has it that at one point in the
construction, a beam of a certain length was needed and
none was found to be long enough. Pedro then ordered a
laborer to take hold of one end while he himself pulled
on the other. To the astonishment of all present, the
beam stretched out to the desired length.

In spite of all these superstitious stories, Pedro
Betancourt must have been a remarkable man. I lament
that the Indians have been taught to kneel before his
tomb, and with lighted candle and prayers, hope he will
perform some miracle on their behalf. I noticed that if
the Indians think Pedro hasn't heard them, they will

knock upon the tomb hoping to call the attention of the dear old saint.

Principle of giving honor to whom honor is due.

Throughout his life Mr. Townsend displayed a special interest and high regard for his host countries' heroes, liberators, statesmen, educators and churchmen who championed the causes of the common man. He was particularly interested in those who spoke up for the ethnic minorities who were generally unable to speak for themselves.

One hero Mr. Townsend admired greatly and sometimes quoted was Bartolomé de las Casas (circa 1500) diplomat, historian, bishop of the state of Chiapas, Mexico, and relentless fighter for the Indian's freedom and justice.

Las Casas was a boy in Spain when Columbus returned from his first voyage. His imagination was fired by the adventures in the New World and he became a Dominican missionary, first to Cuba and then to Mexico. When Las Casas observed the great wickedness and injustices being perpetrated against the Indian, he began a lifelong struggle to champion Indian rights, to secure their freedom from serfdom and to have their lives and property respected. It was his desire that they be treated as ordinary citizens with all the rights and privileges.

Cam's own sense of fair play and Christian charity was often injured when he witnessed inhuman treatment of the ethnic minorities. Yet he chose to do battle for their cause not by militant action that in all probability would have resulted in his expulsion, but by raising the consciousness of those in government and elsewhere of their own national heroes who had introduced plans of reform and justice for the Indian. Cam always remembered that he was a guest in a host country, and that he had come to serve. Thus, over the years, this principle of giving honor to whom honor was due was expanded to include the dictum of one of his early contemporaries, Gilbert H. Grosvenor, Editor-in-Chief of *National Geographic,* who said, "Only what is of a kindly nature is printed [written] about any country, or people. Everything unpleasant or unduly critical is to be avoided."

Another point of interest in Antigua was the ruins of Capuchins. Here one can clearly see the evidences of the cruel inquisition imperishably left in stone. One niche formed the straitjacket into which an offender was fastened while water fell on him drop by drop until he gave in or went mad. There is also a circular building into which monks or nuns were shut in to do penance. Beneath this is a dark dungeon-like chamber whose arched ceiling forms the floor of the building above. It is interesting that the present-day caretaker is a staunch believer in Jesus Christ and has placed Bible House Scripture texts on the walls.

After an exhausting afternoon of exploration, the two men returned to the conference at the Antigua mission. There was another two-hour Bible study by Mr. Bishop, and in the evening, a preaching service conducted by one of the seventeen national workers who were also attending the conference. Cam noted that all of them were fine spiritual men and good preachers. Then Cam wrote about the "fun-maker" of the evening.

Manuel Marroquín had once been a drunken shoemaker before he came to know Jesus Christ. The jail had claimed him as an inmate sixty-three times. Then one day he became interested in the gospel and began to attend church services in town. His wife noticed that her husband began to change some of his habits. He didn't beat her, nor did he come home drunk anymore.

One night, her curiosity aroused, she decided to follow him. To her astonishment, he seemed to be on intimate terms with the hated *evangélicos*. Nevertheless,
she listened at the door and before long she too had
found Jesus as her Lord and Savior.

As the months progressed, Manuel's shoe repair business improved, but one morning he discovered he had
been robbed. Everything had been taken. Manuel then
did an amazing thing. He just praised the Lord and
determined right then and there to give his full time to
the Lord's work, traveling and preaching the gospel.
He couldn't write his name, but he could read and was
a student of the Word. He traveled over much of
Guatemala and El Salvador preaching the Good News
about Jesus Christ and was directly instrumental in
bringing nearly one thousand people into the Kingdom
of God. His sound teaching and jolly manner were a
blessing to all who heard him. Wherever he went, he
was thrown in jail – not for drunkenness, but for his
Master's sake. He could say with Paul, "In stripes, in
imprisonments, in tumults, in labors, in watchings, in
fastings, we are more than conquerors."

As the conference progressed, Cam commented
on the depth of the Bible studies. He recorded that
in Friday's study on Galatians 4:9-11 and Colos-
sians 2:16 the speaker had emphasized that
Christianity should consist of "living in Christ,
not being concerned with observing special days or
ceremonies." The speaker also emphasized the
need for Christians to lay hold of the power that is
within their reach instead of continually praying
for power as many Christians do.

On Saturday, Cam began his diary with the three
words that, in their simplicity, spoke loudly of the

pain he was experiencing in at least one level of this new experience: "Still no mail!" Then with almost a jaunty turn of his pen he wrote, "I forgot to tell you of my first experience at personal work here."

After our Bible study, Mr. Bishop urged us to go out on the streets and do personal work [share their faith]. Even though our Spanish was limited, we determined to set a good example. To cover more ground, Rob and I went out in opposite directions. We had almost no experience in presenting the gospel in English, so that it was doubly hard to try in Spanish. Furthermore, the mere thought of doing it clogged my throat and took my breath away.

I walked down the street about half a block and saw my first man. He was an average-looking man, but as I approached him, my heart was palpitating so hard it kept me from speaking. After going on for another half block, I determined to make another attempt at the man I had passed. Turning around, I walked toward him, but as I drew closer, I was again unable to say a word. And after passing the man three times, I gave up and went on my way.

As I turned the corner, I met a young man very near my own age. This encouraged me, and with a prayer I approached him. We had been told that a good opening question was, "Do you know the Lord Jesus?" At the time I was unaware that the Spanish word for "Lord" may mean either Lord or Mister before a person's name. Many people in Latin America are named "Jesús" (hay-SOOS).

The young man, thinking I had asked, "Do you know Mr. Jesús?" replied, "I am sorry, I can't help you. I am a stranger in town and am not acquainted with the man."

This was too hard a blow for this green colporteur, and I hurriedly made my way back to the safety of the mission.

— 6 —

HERE GOES

During the final days of the conference, Cam and Rob discussed plans for their next month's activity. It was agreed that Rob would work with the Indians in the highland area of Tecpan, thirty miles from Antigua, and Cam would stay in Antigua.

Rob had hoped the mission would provide some sort of transportation – a horse or mule for the long trip out – but as Cam wrote, "They were not about to pamper Rob in any way. However, Rob showed his initiative by securing his own horse for the trip."

Thus after an unexpected early departure by Mr. Bishop and a mid-morning departure by Rob, Cam was left alone with three Spanish-speaking brothers to begin his work as a colporteur.

October 22, 1917. I started right out with my tracts and commenced to work. The majority of the people I met were civil, but a good many pronounced evil benedictions upon this poor *evangélico*, and tore up the tracts. When asked if they believed in Christ, they would invariably reply that they believed in Mary. The women were especially fanatical. A good many that I spoke to were not interested in religion, and one or two seemed to be spiritualists (spiritualism has quite a hold on the middle class).

I get along fairly well in Spanish. I suppose it's because my brogue is humorous. Rob is going to have a harder time because he doesn't know as much Spanish as I do and is going to the least Spanishized Indians. His Cakchiquel Indian worker will be a great help. He was in the States for several years and knows English besides Spanish and his Cakchiquel language. He is a splendid fellow. Not having this kind of help will throw me more on my own resources.

Tuesday, October 23. I was up bright and early and was planning to work in the city when Pastor *Don* Isidro came to my room and asked if I wanted to go to the town of San Antonio, about four-and-a-half hours' walk from here. I told him if I went, I would like to spend a week or so there visiting the eight or nine towns in the area. He said all right, but that it would be wise if I could go today as there were some believers who had missed the stage and wanted to go to San Antonio and Ciudad Viejo, and that we could go along with them. Accordingly, I packed up tracts and things for an eight- or nine-day stay, and we were off by 8:30.

It was a beautiful walk. We passed through coffee plantations and trails that were arched over with amate [wild fig] trees. The small patches of farms are hedged by bamboo fences (chicken tight) or with a stringing of bushes.

Along the way we met a Cakchiquel believer who promised to bring my luggage from Antigua for five pesos (fifteen cents). It weighed about twenty-five or thirty pounds. Further on we met another Cakchiquel believer who promised to go with me on my trip to a neighboring town tomorrow. The Lord sure plans things out fine.

Along the way, *Don* Isidro spoke to several travelers about salvation. He sure is a fine worker. The believers here take it as a matter of course to speak to their
neighbors about the gospel. I am going to learn a lot
from them. I think this year's experience I am having
would be good for every Christian college student whether he goes into full-time service or not.

At the end of our two-hour journey, we passed
through a gap in the mountains and there before us lay
the beautiful valley of San Antonio. A cart road, shaded
by amate trees, hugged the hillside until it reached the
valley below, while a steeper trail for mules and pedes-
trians made the descent more abruptly. To the right
and almost hidden among the foliage, lay the town of
San Antonio. Just beyond, tucked away in the folds of
the hills, nestled San Antonio's companion town, Santa
Catarina.

The cemetery of San Antonio stood out prominently
upon a low hill. Above that there was a trail that scaled
the mountain to two other mountain towns. To the left
of where I stood, and at some distance, was a paradise
of fruit and coffee trees, and like a mirror, sparkled a
lake. Around this were fields and meadows where cattle
grazed. Beyond lay the town of Santiago Samorra. And
at our feet, making a sharp descent around the hill,
went the trail to San Andrecito, just out of sight
around the bend.

As we made our descent into San Antonio, *Don*
Isidro told me a little about one of the men who would
go with me on my trips, where I would sleep and how
my meals would be provided. "Francisco Díaz is a keen-
witted man who loves the Lord. He will be one of your
companions as you pass out tracts in the towns. You
will sleep at the home of an old Indian chief, *Don*
Catarino Lopéz (in his parlor). Your food will be provided by the believers from the town of Santa Catarina."

And that was that. Just as soon as I was introduced to *Don* Catarino, Francisco and a few others, *Don* Isidro and his group left, and once more I was left alone, only this time among a people who spoke very little Spanish. What's more, the people want me to hold meetings at night for the believers for as many nights as I am here. Here goes! We can at least pray and study the Bible and hope that by His grace it will be better than a weak sermon in my poor Spanish.

I am learning to let the Holy Spirit of God into my life more and more, consequently a great many weeds are being choked out that made things miserable for folks around me. I am finding more joy in my work every day.

This afternoon I distributed some tracts and spoke with several, including the mayor. One fellow became real ugly, but a good many listened. At five o'clock I went to have my supper at the hut the believers use as a chapel. After walking over these beautiful hills in this invigorating climate 5,000 feet above sea level, I had developed a hearty appetite! But as I waited in the kitchen where my meal was being prepared, I watched an old Indian woman picking lice off the head of her granddaughter and eating the larger ones. I confess that in the homeland I was somewhat of a finicky eater, and this just about did me in.

I was served my meal – a bowl of soup – on a small wooden table eighteen inches high. When I took my first spoonful, I discovered it was so hot with chile that tears came to my eyes, but smiling, I ate bravely on. I really do like native dishes.

After supper, the believers gathered together for a Bible study in a thatched hut that had been donated for use as a chapel. I was fascinated by how the people crowded into the room. There were about twenty or so. The narrow wooden benches were crowded, and where possible, women and children squatted on woven straw mats spread out on the mud floor.

At the front of the chapel was a rough wooden table that served as a pulpit and stand for the precious paraffin candle – the main source of light. There were some cheaper tallow candles amongst the audience, but after we had finished singing a few hymns, the people, for economy's sake, snuffed them out.

When it came time for me to speak, I peered into the semi-darkness alive with shapes and forms, and where the light from the candle fell, eyes that beamed back at me. Outside the chapel, standing in the doorway, were figures of men who had come to hear but were afraid to come inside. I read John 14, then after a time of prayer, did a study on salvation. The Lord gave me a facility in Spanish greater than I had hoped for (Eph. 3:20). However, I learned some time later that the Indians understood almost nothing of what I said, yet they returned every time I spoke and listened with attention.

Wednesday, October 24. I was up early this morning and managed to get nearly dressed before the family came in to visit me. I had breakfast at the mission shortly after seven, and we were off for Santiago Samora by eight o'clock. It was a beautiful walk among the little plots of grounds called *cuadros* on which the Indians raise their crops. The country reminds me very much of what I have read and heard of Japan – all hilly with volcanoes close at hand. The roads are about twelve feet wide and wind picturesquely over the hills and through the valleys. Trees are everywhere in the valleys and the roads are bordered by the ever-present stinging hedge. The homes are down in the vale, while the *cuadros,* or quarter-acre farms, are on the hillsides. There are generally several homes in a single lot, the families of the second generation having separate thatched huts. They are so surrounded by trees that it is hard at first to know whether you are walking through a farm or a town. Most of the men speak some Spanish, but the women do not. When I encounter one that can't speak any more Spanish than myself, I have my companion present the gospel in the Cakchiquel language. I can tell pretty well what he's talking about because he mixes in a good bit of Spanish, especially for religious words.

The town of Santiago has about one hundred (sometimes three or four families to a home) and we were through before eleven o'clock. Since it is just a half-hour's walk back to Santa Catarina, we arrived in time for *almuerzo* [lunch]. We didn't encounter a great deal of opposition, but a good many refused to listen to us and others tore up our tracts. We undertook to give the essentials of the gospel to all we met. My companion, Jóse María Sackche, was a great help. He was always ready to present the truth in the Cakchiquel language if they didn't understand my Spanish.

We were off again at one o'clock for San Lorenzo el Cubo, another half-hour's walk. Here we encountered a little more opposition, but we had a very blessed afternoon, getting back shortly after four o'clock. We missed very few houses, if any. Supper, or *comida*, was served up almost immediately and afterwards I prepared for the meeting in the evening.

The men began to gather soon after six and held a discussion amongst themselves while waiting for seven o'clock and the beginning of the meeting. One of the women brought in some coffee and rolls for me. They sure are kind folks. They won't take a cent for my grub and wouldn't let me help pay for the candles. I don't know what I can do about the coffee. I get tired of refusing, and they don't understand it. It's very weak, however, and I think purer than what we can get at home, so I don't think it will hurt me much. It is very good, although it doesn't have any milk in it. We had a fine meeting. The singing is a fright, but they seem to enjoy it. I am by far the best singer in the bunch! *Nuff sed.*

Jóse María is more *castellano* [taken to Spanish ways] than any of the rest. They say he can preach well in Spanish and in Cakchiquel. They all seem to respect him. He told me that he was a musician but when he was converted he quit his business as it threw him in too much with unbelievers. He wants to go to the States and work until he can get enough money to take piano or organ lessons. My favorite is a fellow by the name of Francisco Díaz. He is about thirty-five, handsome and stalwart, with an intelligent wide-awake face.

Thursday, October 25. This morning we were off early for the town of Dueñas, about three miles distant. It was as beautiful a walk as I have ever taken. The volcano Agua rose up high to the left and majestic Fuego stood out unclouded far above the farm-covered hills to the right. Below us in the valley was a lake surrounded by broad meadows where several herds of cattle were feeding. All was beautiful without and joy within. With every step, I thanked God for the joy of life and service. The mayor at Dueñas was most favorable to the gospel and took a New Testament. We also met the *comandante* of Ciudad Viejo who was making a visit and he asked me to go over there tomorrow. They say that it is close enough to go over in an hour. That is probably the field for tomorrow and Saturday.

As we moved about the town, we met an old woman who, when I gave her a tract, asked for more. As Francisco and I explained the gospel to her, she suddenly tore up the tracts and then offered me a Catholic leaflet of her own. I smiled and accepted it. It offered me, the sinner, 500 days of special dispensation.

Later that morning, while we were talking to a group

in the street about the way of salvation, a woman came out of a nearby hut and began to rail and curse us with all her might. As we passed her house, Francisco Díaz who accompanied me, said we had better pass on as the son was the altar boy in the church. I saw him standing by the gate, however, and thought that he ought to have a chance to read the gospel as much as anyone else. Accordingly,I offered him a tract, but he began a devilish tirade and the first thing we knew, was throwing stones at us. Fortunately, none of them hit us, and it made me happy that we could partake in a little bit, at least, of what Paul and the early disciples experienced.

A native worker of Mr. Bishop's was expected to come and preach tonight but he didn't show up and I had to prepare another study while eating a splendid supper. Thirty attended the meeting tonight and we had a fine time.

After Bible study and prayer, Francisco told of our day's experiences. I could follow him pretty well by the Spanish he mixed in with Cakchiquel. He dwelt at length upon the mayor's favorable reception of the gospel, the stoning, and my blessing the two women who tore up the tracts in our presence while pronouncing curses upon us. I am afraid he got our listeners a little scared when he said the *comandante* had refused to be responsible if anything happened when we tried to distribute tracts here in San Antonio. This made them hesitant about offering to accompany me, but I reassured them, and I think they will all help distribute here next Sunday.

They have all been so kind that I have decided to give one-tenth of my twenty-five dollars to pay half the expenses of one of the children at the mission school at Guatemala if they care to pay the other half. They took up the matter and will let me know before I leave. They need education, especially the women along sanitary lines and health in general.

This evening, *Don* Catarino, in whose home I sleep, promised to loan me a horse every day hereafter. He said he would have offered it before except he had been upset over a shot that had been fired into his bedroom through the window the night before I arrived. I think the believers are mighty fine Christians considering they are only a few months old in their faith.

Friday, October 26. This morning I breakfasted as usual on coffee and rolls, and by 7:45 I was in the saddle and off for Ciudad Viejo with my companion of the day, Felipe Hernandez. The *comandante* received us cordially and showed great interest in the gospel. He said he was glad to see our literature distributed as it would bring the people out of their ignorance and superstition. Ciudad is a city of 6,000 and we put in a hard day. We were met by the usual cry, "We believe only in the *Santísima Virgen.*"

Several listened attentively to the gospel and seemed to be under conviction. Little can be done, however, unless you can talk alone with the person. One woman showed considerable interest in the Word but suddenly began to yell about the "Most Holy Virgin." I found that a group of her neighbors had gathered at the gate and since she couldn't make her children understand by motions that she wanted the gate closed, had to put on a Catholic front. They must think the tracts are poisonous, for it is very difficult to persuade some to take them. When they see us coming, a few of the women gather their children about them and run down the street as though the devil were after them.

I was pretty tired this evening but a good meal at *Don* Catarino's (the best I've had yet – three eggs and beans with five tortillas accompanied by coffee, which I had just before declined) put me in shape for the service and we had a good time. I expect to go to Alotenango tomorrow. It is a six- or eight-mile ride each way, so I will not be able to have a meeting tomorrow as I will be too tired. It is a city of about two thousand. I will finish Ciudad Viejo the day that I return to Antigua as it is not far off the road. At last a letter from home! Thanks Ethel.

Saturday, October 27. *Don* Catarino's son accompanied me today. He is only nine years old and was in the saddle almost all day, but didn't complain a bit. We went through Dueñas and then along the foot of Fuego (the highest volcano in Central America). Most of the way lay along the *finca* (or farm) Capitilla. Up on the mountainside were a few plots that belonged to the Cakchiquels, but most of the land between the volcanoes Fuego and Agua belongs to the one farm. There were great fields of corn, coffee and sugar cane, while around Lake San Antonio were broad pastures where many herds were feeding. The owner's country residence and the main buildings of the farm are encountered just before one reaches Alotenango. There is a large sugar mill run by water power. Across the creek from these buildings is a good-sized village of thatched huts where the employees live. The employees are practically permanent fixtures of a farm for as long as they live because the owner manages to keep them in debt to him loaning them money when they are broke during the season when there is no work, and then pays them only six pesos (eighteen cents) per day when there is work. There is a law to force debtors to work, and it is enforced by the government with rigidity, especially on the Indians.

While Alotenango has a pretty location nestled between the volcanoes Agua and Fuego, it is the most miserable little city I've seen in these parts. Many of the streets are nothing but gulleys or mountain trails, and the people are poor and illiterate. Few could read and those who could were afraid to take the tracts. We had a very good day, however, despite the fact that one of the numerous dogs bit a hole in my corduroys. I walked right on into the yard, trusting the Lord would take him off and the cur let go without drawing blood. This is the fourth or fifth time that Ethel's [one of Cam's four older sisters] sewing kit has come in handy.

I learned a lasting and important lesson from this experience. I was unaware of the Indian custom of stopping at the gate of a house and calling before entering the yard. My practice has been to walk right into a yard and offer a tract to the Indian people who, I've noticed, were often quite scared. Then I would quote John 3:16 and offer as much of an explanation as my limited command of Spanish would allow, then walk out. From now on I'll be sure to call out before entering.

Principle of cultural awareness and practical use of anthropology.

The pervading mission opinion during Cam's day as a colporteur often considered a particular culture's behavior as something to be modified to be more like a Western, or American lifestyle and mindset. Mr. Townsend, on the other hand, recognized early in his ministry that the Cakchiquel people were different from Americans and indeed differed in beliefs, customs, art forms and, of course, language from other ethnic minorities in Guatemala. Therefore, instead of fighting this difference or treating Cakchiquel customs as somehow inferior to his own, Cam appreciated these cultural diversities and sought to understand and view them from a practical or anthropological point of view. He accepted the differences as a gift of God's common grace for the enrichment of all.

One way Mr. Townsend championed the ethnic minorities was by encouraging and sponsoring living museums* where people of all ethnic backgrounds might come together to both learn and enjoy the rich heritage of a cross-cultural experience.

On Sunday, October 28, Cam wrote that he rose early in order to "whip a sermon into shape."

It was really my first attempt at a sermon, in either English or Spanish. The other meetings have been more in the nature of Bible studies and prayer meetings. From Genesis 8:22, I tried to talk on certain laws of God as found in nature. Then I mentioned a few spiritual laws we should know and observe if we are to live our lives regulated according to God's standard. I used such Scriptures as Romans 6:23, Ezekiel 18:4, 2 Peter 3:9, John 4:24, Exodus 20:4-7, and Psalms 51:17. I also used Matthew 7:13 and suggested that we ought not to expect to be popular and go with the crowd.

My sermon lasted three-fourths of an hour and although I slaughtered Spanish frightfully, they seemed to follow pretty well.

It was a full and exciting Sunday, and later that night, Cam wrote home.

Sunday, October 28, 1917

Dear Home Folks,

I received Ethel's letter Friday and one today. Six weeks without hearing from home is a long time. I hope hereafter letters will arrive more frequently. I am having a great time out here with the Indians. I am in beautiful country snugly situated between the famous

---

*SIL and WBT have three principal museums in the United States: the Museum of Anthropology in Dallas, Texas, and the Museum of the History of Alphabets and the Mexico-Cardenas Museum in Waxhaw, North Carolina.

volcanoes Agua and Fuego. By tomorrow evening I will
have worked quite thoroughly six towns from one
hundred to six thousand population. The Lord has been
with me all the way. For the next ten or twelve days I
will work around Antigua and go to Chimaltenango and
work in that area.

I will attend a missionary conference in Guatemala
City from November 25 to December 29. In January I
will work in Santa Cosa (I am hoping to work along the
coastal areas in the cooler months). After that I plan to
go to Jutiapa which borders on El Salvador and Honduras, and then to Jalapa.

I am fortunate to be able to attend two more confer-
ences on the field, and during Lent, the big conference
of the year in Guatemala City. After this, I will probably leave for a four-month trip through Mexico. For the
present and keeping an eye on the future, I am putting
forth every effort to give a good report of myself. The
rainy season is just about over. December and January
are the cold months; March and April the hot ones. The
climate here at four to five thousand feet is as delightful as the scenery. Living has been very inexpensive.
During this past week, the Indian believers have furnished meals, candles and room free.

> There were several more paragraphs in the letter
> that dealt with the instructions for the chayotes
> (vine-type vegetable) that he would send later.
> Then in his characteristically jaunty tone, Cam
> signed off with, "*Buenas noches.* Bushels of love,
> Cameron." There was a P.S. to Fleet (his sister's
> husband) who had a new job to whom Cam said,
> "Congratulations. Do it up brown."

— 7 —

EARLY TRIALS

Almost from the moment of his arrival in San Antonio (the town's full name is San Antonio Aguas Calientes), Cam developed a special affection for the Cakchiquel Indian believers, and for the quaint village itself. He ended his first week there expressing confidence in God and great delight in how the Lord had led him during the events of that past week. The one particular event that Cam said was the most blessed day in his memory, took place on Friday in a beer garden in the town of Viega, a few miles from San Antonio.

I had decided to carry the gospel wherever I thought there was a need. Accordingly, when my companion and I spotted a kind of beer garden, we went inside. Here I saw a Cakchiquel Indian man drinking. After speaking with him for a few moments, I offered him a Gospel of John. He refused. I smiled, and with my companion, we left the beer garden and began to walk down the street. We hadn't gone very far when suddenly we heard someone running after us. It was the man from the beer garden.

"I can't read," he said, "but if you give me the book, I will find someone who can read it for me." I gladly gave him a Gospel together with a cordial invitation to attend the service to be held in the Santa Catarina chapel on Sunday. Later that night, I asked the believers to pray for this man.

To Cam's surprise, the man came to the service. When Cam gave an invitation at the conclusion of his sermon, the man stood, indicating he wanted to accept the Lord.

His name is Tiburcio. Afterward the Indian believers explained the gospel more fully to him in the Cakchiquel language, then prayed with him. Even though Tiburcio was still somewhat intoxicated, he seemed to understand the new commitment he had made. He then left for his home five miles away.

Cam didn't see Tiburcio again for several years but faithfully prayed that he would become established in his faith. God answered Cam's prayers in a remarkable way. Tiburcio had drunk heavily most of his life. However, he was never to become drunk again. He had made a life commitment to follow Jesus Christ, and this meant living his life in a way that would honor his new Master. While this pleased Tiburcio's wife and children, it did not rest well with his community.

Tiburcio's community demanded that its male inhabitants drink with one another. Local store or land owners encouraged drunkenness as a sure way to secure the Indians' indebtedness to them, thereby assuring them of virtual slave labor. Therefore, when Tiburcio's lifestyle changed and he no longer involved himself in excessive drinking, his friends ridiculed him. In desperation, some threw liquor over him with the hope that the smell would once again quicken his desire. It did not. And there were other kinds of threats. Once he was attacked by a

machete-wielding bigot who accused him of being
in league with the devil for becoming an *evangélico*. Yet through it all, Tiburcio remained faithful
to his Lord.

Impressed with Tiburcio's new lifestyle, particularly with the way he was systematically paying
back his debts, the landowner to whom he was in
debt gave Tiburcio a position of overseer and responsibility on his plantation. It didn't matter to
him that Tiburcio didn't know how to read or
write. The owner recognized an honesty that
hadn't been there before. Tiburcio never learned to
read, but his two daughters did; they were taught
by the mission school teachers from the Presbyterian Girl's School.

Years later, when Mr. Townsend recalled the incident, he said: "Tiburcio was a great inspiration
to me. When I learned of all he endured because of
his faith, yet never tired of telling others about
what Christ had done for himself and his family, I
thought about the time we walked into that beer
garden. I learned from that experience that God
could take a poor instrument like me, and if the
instrument was willing, lead that person into a
place of need for the honor and glory of Himself."

October 28, 1917. The believers wanted another
meeting this afternoon and so after I and a brother who
had come all the way from Alotenango had distributed
our tracts in a small town nearby, we met together for a
Bible study.

After the meeting, I found it hard to say good-bye to
the Indians. They are a fine bunch of Christians! I don't
suppose I'll ever get to see them again this side of heaven. However, one amazing thing has happened. Francisco Díaz [Frisco] and I have become fast friends. He

has promised to give up farming his little hillside plot of ground and accompany me as my carrier and helper. He will, in all probability, become my mentor. However, he won't be able to start until December.

I will leave in the morning for Antigua. I plan to work several hours in the town of Vieja and along the road. It is about a seven- or eight-mile walk from San Antonio back to Antigua. I ought to get husky at this rate!

As we left the Bible study, I saw a drunken woman lying in the street. Quite a crowd had gathered and a policeman was just arriving. They have no patrol wagons here and a cop with an ancient rifle impressed a couple of men to carry her to the jail. She proved to be too heavy, so they dragged her.

If too many brothers don't call on me, I'm going to get some letters written tonight as they will have to go in the mail tomorrow. Today is the Fiesta of Minerva. A marimba was going nearly all last night and all day today. It is pretty music, but I should think that the players would get tired. It is something like a xylophone except that it is all wood and there are three players. It sounds halfway between a piano and a full orchestra, if you can imagine that. *Don* Catarino just told me that he was going to loan me a horse again tomorrow. He is a great old scout. I forgot to say that Minerva Day is a sort of a universal graduation day for all the schools. The children get out and march, etc.

Tuesday, October 30. Last night I played the little organ for the audience to sing by! I'll never agonize them again, whether they strike the tune or not. How I wish I had minded Mama and practiced when I had a chance!

This morning Pastor *Don* Isidro accompanied me to the town of San Pedro de las Huertas. He was the spokesman. He is a fine worker and interested a number in the gospel. I learned a lot of good methods and had opportunity to hear Spanish as it should be spoken. I think he will accompany me most of the rest of the week. We took *almuerzo* (light lunch) with the only believer there, the foreman of a coffee plantation who is paid thirteen pesos a day, or thirty-four cents. The laborers only get six pesos (seventeen cents). In the afternoon we stopped again on our return and they treated us to boiled squash. It was good but should have been baked and the strings taken out. We walked home in a light rain.

This evening I started out to get sugar and nuts to make some candy, but only one store has nuts, and it was closed. In my quest for walnuts, I met a young druggist I had met once before who had invited me to dinner. I had to refuse then, but now felt I should accept his invitation. He speaks English (there are only three or four in Antigua who can) and it was quite pleasant. He has given the gospel much consideration, but he has ideas that get him nowhere. He has heard too much denominationalism here as well as in New Orleans where he lived some time. It has served to disgust him with the plain gospel.

Wednesday, October 31. This morning we hiked over to San Felipe, a town of about two hundred population. We went into a banana *finca* (plantation) and tried to interest the lady of the house in a *"Porciones Escogidas,"* (Selected Portions) but nothing doing! She believed in God all right, but told us it wasn't good to read that kind of literature. Just as she was showing us the gate, the man came out, and in about two minutes, *Don* Isidro had sold him a book. *Don* Isidro follows the policy of offering the "Portions Selected from the Word of God" for sale at a very low price – four *reals*, or 1½ cents. The book is interesting and illustrated and allows him to give the gospel message while showing the book. It also gives a chance to see whether the party would really like to read the Word or not. If the party shows interest but hasn't the money, I give them a gospel or tract.

We try to get every family to take a tract, but in some towns a great many tear them up. In Dueñas we could trace most of our way around town by torn tracts. The people are told it is a sin for them to read or even listen to *evangélico* propaganda. Sometimes we are given produce in exchange for the book. Yesterday a woman gave us three roasting ears of corn. She was deeply interested. I pray she won't regret her bargain.

In the afternoon we worked there in Antigua but I don't think we accomplished much. There are a great many Mexican prelates here now as exiles from Mexico. They assist in propagating fanaticism. I felt a little down in my spirits this evening but a letter from home and one from my sister Lula has completely recharged me with pep. I think the letters must have gone by way of San Francisco for they were a long time getting here.

The pastor's daughter had some candy for us tonight. It seems the stores have plenty of peanuts, but no imported nuts. At any rate, she had gotten peanuts, and with the sugar I had bought, prepared some dandy candy. With the letter, it went fine.

For the next two weeks, Cam made short day trips out from Antigua into the surrounding villages, towns and countryside. Sometimes he was accompanied by *Don* Isidro, and on other occasions, worked the surrounding towns alone.

No two days were exactly the same, and while each encounter had a certain sameness, there was in each a God-directed drama. It was a drama played out as a spectacle before a grandstand of angelic powers who were watching the complex

wisdom of God's eternal plan for Cameron Townsend being worked out among the day-to-day dis-
couragements, defeats, joys and victories of his
beginning days in Guatemala.

The New Testament Book of James says test-
ings that come to the believer's faith develop in
him fortitude (patient courage under affliction,
manliness). In order for Cam to gain the fortitude
needed to develop his moral leadership and his
celebrated unflinching resolve for worldwide Bible
translation, these early trials were in reality friends
to be welcomed and embraced. One had a faint
similarity to Joseph's experience with Potiphar's
wife (Genesis 39).

Friday, November 2. This morning we were awakened
by the ringing of bells all over the city. The racket kept
up with few cessations most all day. They say it is a
fiesta in honor of the dead, or All Saints' Day. At any
rate, no one is supposed to work. The Indians get drunk
and the women decorate the graves in the cemetery.
Despite all the excitement, we had great success. Seventeen or eighteen families purchased portions of Scripture and a good many listened attentively to the Word.
In the afternoon, *Don* Isidro was busy with the Indians
from San Antonio who are undergoing considerable persecution; therefore, I went out alone. I am getting to the
place where I can speak Spanish well enough to be
understood by most of the people. I sold nine Scripture
portions and one Testament. I think one of the men I
talked with is on the verge of accepting Christ. If we
depend absolutely on the Lord we can accomplish lots,
but if we go out in our own strength, it's all failure and
discouragement.

I was almost taken in at one home where there were
three pretty *señoritas* in the family. The mother bought
a book and wanted me to come in for refreshments. She

also said if I was staying at a hotel, I could have a room with her for as long as I stayed in Antigua. They had a beautiful coffee *finca* right next to some old ruins, but it was a good bit more dangerous than the stones of Dueñas. I quickly left, even refusing the refreshments!

It is cold here now. Brother Paul's sweater comes in mighty handy. I don't know how Rob likes it way up on the mountains at Tecpan. The wind is blowing tonight and that is a sure sign that the rains are over.

November 3. We had one of the most beautiful walks yet this morning. The way led out due south of town through an ancient *alameda,* or avenue, over a hundred feet in width and shaded by a row of gigantic trees on either side that resembled the oaks of Montevista. This led to an ancient monastery in front of which was a cross of stone some fifteen feet high, bearing the date 1729. At intervals along the way were the remains of massive-walled, one-celled prisons where hermits had penanced away their lives. From the monastery, the road diverged somewhat to the left and lay between beautiful coffee *fincas.* We met several oxcarts and a number of Indians carrying produce to the market in Antigua. One had brought bananas twenty-two miles from Palin. They weren't as big as the kind we generally get in the States, but they had a mighty fine flavor. I ate four and a half myself!

San José is quite a ways up on the slope of old Agua and from the municipal building we had a beautiful view of Antigua and the surrounding valley. It is certainly a beautiful garden spot. We passed an old stone pile which they think dates back to the Spanish invasion. Our lunch consisted of four tortillas that we had received in exchange for a Scripture portion, the bananas, a rock to sit on, and a beautiful view upon which to look. We had a good day and got back to the mission a little before four. I had a wonderful meal of meat and black beans all mashed up like jam.

I am interested in the different ways we are being received as we travel the countryside. One man told me he was past eighty and even though he couldn't read, he wasn't "going to be fooled by any upstart," like me. One woman made fun of us for associating with poor people, to which I replied that Christ Himself was poor.

On the other hand, we met many who expressed true interest in the gospel. One man paid for his New Testament with a big squash. Others gave us roasting ears of corn and some gave us fruit. In the town of Santa Magdalena, I was given a military escort to guide me around town. The mayor then received me in his vegetable garden. He was barefoot and wasn't able to read. Inside his hut he had a statue of the town saint which was his responsibility during his time in office.

In one hamlet, everyone came out to see what we were selling. The reason was because a girl ran from house to house crying, *"Evangélicos, evangélicos!"* Everyone was terribly frightened.

Cam's trip to San José was particularly interesting. After a long climb up the side of the great volcano, Cam, in the company of several Cakchiquel Indian workers, first met the town officials. Afterward the Indian workers addressed the crowd that had gathered. Later Cam and the workers went from house to house.

After listening to the gospel message conducted in Cakchiquel, Cam noted that the Indians would fold their hands and with uplifted eyes say, *"Matiosh chiri Dios"* (thanks be to God). However, Cam was not as pleased with the presentation as the Indian believers appeared to be.

Don Lucas spoke in Cakchiquel, therefore I was unable to understand most of what he said. There were,

however, just enough Spanish words mixed in to make
me warn *Don* Lucas of two serious mistakes he was
making. First, he told the people I came from a country
where everyone spoke Latin. His surprise was great
when I told him Latin is a dead language. And his second mistake was his remark that since God made
women from the rib of man, man has one less rib than
woman. I felt this was an awful mistake considering the
many odd tales that are widely circulated and believed
by so many Indians. One of these has to do with the
creation of women, and goes as follows: God caused
Adam to fall into a deep sleep. He then took a rib out of
Adam's side and laid it on the grass while He closed up
Adam's wound. While God was doing this, a little dog
came along and snapped up the rib. God noticed this
just in time to grab the dog's tail. The dog escaped, but
left his tail in God's hand. God's only recourse now was
to make Eve out of the dog's tail, which he proceeded
to do.

This story is generally believed among the people and
is shown by the servile position women are given. I suppose I should not be too hard on *Don* Lucas. He does,
after all, preach Christ and Him crucified, and on Sunday morning when he preached, seven Indians professed their faith in Christ.

> Cam's journals and diaries mirrored in amazing
> detail his daily routine. But it was his letters to
> his parents and friends that revealed his true
> humanity and feelings.

November 4, 1917

Dear Home Folks,

I was sure glad to get your letters and the news that
you received my letter from Manzanillo, Mexico. I was
a little afraid the officials might feel hurt at the way I
spoke of soldiers. I hope none of my letters miscarry

any negative feelings for any of the things I am seeing down here.

I am wondering where your Thanksgiving dinner will be held this year. I expect to eat mine in Guatemala City with the missionaries. It will be the last day of the conference and I am anticipating this with considerable pleasure.

How is the football team doing this year? Paul, can't you take time to write me a long letter and tell me about your college courses, your first impressions with the faculty, Y.M.C.A., lit., societies, etc., the number that have been drafted and everything in general?

Time is certainly flying down here. In a few more days I will be through with Antigua, then a week around Chimaltenango and another around Santiago and then the missionary conference in Guatemala City. I am enjoying every day. It is a great training school and the Lord is blessing me. The only thing that I don't like is the cold. The wind has been blowing the last two days and it seems cold enough to freeze. I was meant for a warm climate.

I have an appetite for everything here – especially black beans. I think I will send some to you to see if they will grow in California. I have a dandy room at the mission and sometimes I can hardly believe I am on the mission field for I have found hardship in nothing. The poor Indian believers are undergoing considerable hardship because of their faith. I am afraid the church in the States doesn't know what persecution is.

One of the problems with the local church here is that it has sought to be popular and follow the demands of the crowd rather than follow the teaching of Scripture. It has won ascendancy here on earth but lost its place in heaven. We must remember that if we are followers of Christ, the world will hate us because it hated Christ.

Don't forget to write. A letter from home is worth
its weight in gold down here.

Love to all,
Cameron

— 8 —

MOVING OUT

Cam's letter to the "home folks" dated November 12, 1917 spoke about visiting twenty-one different towns in twenty-two days. To some of these towns he traveled on horseback; to others on bicycle (he noted that this was quite a novelty), but mostly he traveled by foot.

In his letter, he also asked about his father's registered sow and wanted to know if indeed pureblood pigs sold for a higher price than non-registered stock. If they sold well, he added, he hoped some of the money could be used to make his life insurance payment.

Speaking of money, he asked if the ladies missionary society could assume partial support of the ten-year-old daughter of his Indian helper in order to send her to the mission school. "It will cost two and a half dollars per month for nine months," he wrote. If the missions society could do this much, he would pay the other half out of his wages. Cam assured his parents that he had quite enough money to assume this responsibility.

Principle of seeing beyond needs to possibilities.

Throughout his long life, Mr. Townsend or Uncle

Cam, as the Wycliffe family and his many friends were to call him, looked for ways to help certain people whom he met to reach their potential, often through higher education. The most notable among the many whom Cam helped where Elena Trejo and Mary Johnson.* Elena was a young illiterate Cakchiquel girl who became a competent physician. Mary is a Bible translator with her husband for the Secoya people in Ecuador.

November 13, 1917. I had everything ready this morning to leave the mission at seven o'clock and move to Chimaltenango, but the carrier didn't show up. In that my boxes were too heavy for a carrier to take in one trip, I decided to wait for an oxcart from Chimaltenango. I worked two hours with *Don* Manuel in Antigua, and then went down to where the Camino Real enters the city from Chimaltenango. The Lord had a cart waiting for me and after a little bartering they agreed to bring over my luggage for sixteen pesos. After a fine *almuerzo* (all my meals at the mission in Antigua were splendid, thanks to the pastor's daughter), I hit the trail afoot for Chimaltenango. However, I missed the most direct road, and arrived in three hours and ten minutes.

Chimaltenango sits on a broad plateau over a range of hills from Antigua. It is considerably higher, and colder. The products are corn, beans and bricks. A person misses the coffee groves of Antigua and yet I enjoy being in an open country, for it seems more like home. I felt sorry that the *mozo* [hired hand] went back on me. He was the Indian Mr. Bishop had picked out to accompany me and I had intended to try him out for ten days in Chimaltenango and Santiago. If he can't be depended upon, I thank the Lord for letting me know

---

*See *Never Touch A Tiger,* by Hugh Steven (Thomas Nelson Publishers, 1980), p. 58 ff.

this early in the game. I think He certainly led me in securing Francisco. The pastor won't be home here at Chimaltenango until Saturday, so one of the members is going to accompany me.

I have a nice little room with a hard wood bed. I unpacked my stuff with the assistance of the whole family and I almost forgot that I liked children. I hit the hay early these nights, and so "good night everybody."

Wednesday, November 14. I've hit another military town – San Andrés Iztapa. At various hours of the night, the bugler showed that he was awake by a spasm of violent tooting. Thank goodness the six-man arsenal at Antigua didn't have a fife and drum corps. The pastor's wife had a hard time getting the stove to work this morning. In the better houses, the stoves are concrete grates occupying the whole side of the kitchen. Of course, they all burn wood or, if it can be afforded, charcoal. They are hard to start and make little heat. The cook has an awfully hard job in this country. *Doña* Aurora, however, doesn't believe in making a fellow work on rolls and coffee, and I got a dish of beans for breakfast.

We worked today in Iztapa. It is quite a distance away and it took over an hour of fast walking to get there. There is an Indian believer there and we had our preliminary quiet hour in his home. His wife also prepared us a fine *almuerzo* for five pesos (thirteen cents). The town is very fanatical. One woman, a saloon keeper, burnt the tract she had received while we were talking to her. At one time quite a crowd (it was really an angry mob) gathered in the streets and called us devils and threatened to have us arrested. Sure enough, about five o'clock as we were talking with some men just before leaving the town, down the street came six soldiers. The lieutenant wanted to know if we had the *"boleto de ornato."* I told him that we carried only a limited supply of books, but that he could look them over. My companion, however, sensed the situation and told the officer that we didn't have the aforesaid *boleto*. He then ordered us to accompany him to see the mayor, which we did.

The mayor was a big fellow, more or less under the influence of liquor. He began talking to me, but as I didn't know what the *"boleto"* was, all I could do was to tell him about our work. Something my companion said didn't please him and he shouted to the soldiers, "Throw these fellows in jail." They didn't obey, however, and after a few words of explanation on the part of José, he proceeded to write out a *boleto* for José. A *boleto* is something like a poll tax receipt that every citizen is supposed to carry. José didn't have his, so it cost nine pesos, half of which was in the way of a fine. I won't need one until I've been here a year. He tried to make out that I was a German (the Germans are now under strict surveillance here), but I had little trouble in establishing my nationality. With the application of a few *"su servidores"* (your servant), he settled down and listened to the gospel and even received some tracts. I suppose we should have visited him in the first place.

Principle of observing correct protocol.

Of all the experiences Cam had during his first years in Guatemala, this incident gave rise to one of the most important and significant of all Wycliffe and SIL working principles. It was the principle of starting at the top, nationally and locally, and keeping the government informed about what you are doing. Said Dick Pittman,* "It was an important lesson in protocol or ordered rules, of

*Dr. Pittman later succeeded Mr. Townsend as SIL's director in Mexico and later as the Asia Area Director.

observing the proper sequence of events, like the correct order ingredients are introduced into a cake batter to make it work. A high official does not appreciate learning via the grapevine that a visitor has arrived and is seeing those under him before seeking to see him."

Thursday, November 15. Today we were able to work the two towns of San Miguel and Tejar as they were close together. José Arroyo again accompanied me. He is a young fellow of twenty-two years, recently converted. Although he has been a believer less than six months, he is well-versed in the Bible and as a personal worker. I like him better than the regular pastors I have worked with. He is anxious to devote his whole time to the work and only $7.50 a month would put him in the field as colporteur and personal worker. We were well received in both San Miguel and Tejar. Many showed great interest.

We ate our lunch under a big tree next to the *pila*. The *pila* is the village fountain, watering trough and wash tub. It is built of concrete, in two parts. The first is immediately under the spout for dipping drinking water. The overflow from this goes to the watering trough from which the women also dip water for washing their clothes. There are generally concrete scrubbing boards on each side of the trough. Here the women wash the clothes, often without soap. The grass around the *pila* serves as the clothesline. In Ciudad Viejo there was only one good *pila* where fifteen to thirty women could be seen at most any time of the day washing their clothes.

Supper was ready when I got home. I got up from the table to give some tracts to an Indian believer from a village twelve miles away, and before I was through with him, prayer meeting was started. I don't get much time to write or read.

Friday, November 16. I am getting my fill of black beans. The other evening, after a strenuous day, I was served a two-course meal. The first was a dish of black beans with tortillas. The second was a dish of black beans covered with sour cream. I received the first dish gratefully, and the second would have been received with just as much gratitude, if it hadn't been that I saw, just that morning, the cream standing in a dirty jar and full of flies. But these discomforts count for little in the joy of the work.

This morning we had a hard walk of an hour and a quarter over gullies, through bean fields to the town of Parramos. The most remarkable thing about Parramos is its broad streets. They are nearly one hundred feet wide and cross at right angles. Even in the heart of the town, each house had a large orchard and garden around it. There were many alligator pear trees which grow to be like our mighty oaks.

We had a splendid day. A large part of the population was Indian and some treated us poorly. One fellow saw us come out of the pasture where we had been praying previous to entering the city. I offered him a tract and started to talk to him, but he laughed like a crazy person and ran down the street shouting, "Oh, I know you, you're *evangélicos, evangélicos!*" It reminded us of the girl with the evil spirit in Philippi. His cries, however, brought a congregation around us and gave us a good opportunity to preach the Word. Another woman wouldn't listen to us at all but just kept saying, "*La Virgen y nada más*" [the virgin and nothing else].

An Indian woman said we were *evangélicos* and sent her daughter on the run to tell the *comandante*. Just before noon we found a woman who claimed to be a believer who warmed our tortillas and made us coffee (I have nearly succeeded in getting the cooks to serve me hot water instead of coffee). The pastor's wife says the woman professed at one time but now her husband has turned spiritualist and has nothing to do with the church. This evening I had beans again for supper. If I don't get them twice a day here in Chimaltenango, it is three times a day. They are good, but a fellow can even get too much pie!

Saturday, November 17. This morning a young baker accompanied me here in Chimaltenango. We found a great deal of interest especially among the Indians. The spiritual condition of the people here reminds me of Mark 7:6-8. They all profess to be Christians, but they know nothing of what the term should mean. To them, it merely means that they adhere to the Roman Catholic Church. This afternoon I took a day off. After getting off my weekly epistle home, I followed José to a barber shop. I hadn't had a haircut since the 11th of September in Oakland and I was really afraid to go on to the capital without one. I was nearly as afraid of risking the barber shop, but José said it was a good one, so I went. A haircut and a mock shampoo costs five pesos, or 12½ cents. He nearly emptied his perfume bottle on me and in appreciation of his goodwill, I tipped him two pesos. We then tried to find an oxcart to haul my things to Guatemala next week, but without success. A circus came to town on the sly today (I didn't see a single advertisement of it and ran upon it by accident), but nothing can tempt me away from bed these nights.

Sunday, November 18. *Doña* Aurora told me this morning that we had five earthquakes last night that toppled over a few houses in nearby towns. It's strange I didn't awaken. This morning the plaza was full of Indians who are journeying to the capital to take part in the festivals prior to the president's birthday. Many were entire families. They carried their blankets and food on their backs, and cooked and slept in the plaza.

Sunday morning is the time for military instruction. Nearly all the men have to train in this department for military preparedness. In that this is the department capital, the men came in to drill this morning from all the neighboring towns. The Ladinos [westernized Spanish-speaking Latin Americans], drilled with guns while the Indians, guarded by armed soldiers, exercised with hoes. There were scarcely a dozen amongst the whole number, Ladinos and Indians, who wore shoes. The captain gave me permission to hand out tracts to the men.

I also talked with Indian travelers in the plaza. Today is the big market day, too. All the shops keep open. This afternoon, the Indian believer from Iztapa accompanied me on another house-to-house canvas. He had come in with his family for the service, but I thought that the work was more important and persuaded him to accompany me. Nearly all the population of this city is Indian and it is hard for them to understand Spanish, let alone my brand. The Indians are more or less afraid of us and few can read. Their condition is lamentable. Nearly all have their idols. Their economic condition is as bad. They get only five or six pesos (15 cents) a day when they work. They live on corn and beans and if these should fail, they would be in the throes of famine. It is a country without a capital. Unless there is a Chinese merchant in town, it is practically impossible to change a twenty-five peso (60 cent) bill. There are only one or two banks outside of the capital. The average store has far less in quantity and variety than Mother's pantry. Women go to the store to buy 2/3 cents' worth of sugar or a tablespoon full of lard. Such luxuries as candy can be found only in the larger cities, and then there are only one or two kinds. If a *mozo* can raise enough corn and beans to do him the year around, he is all right. He can even afford to over-indulge in *aguardiente* (booze) every Saints' Day. If for any reason his crop fails, he is at famine's door. Many of the *fincas* pay only three pesos (7½ cents) a day. I don't see how they can live on it. My beans and tortillas cost me seven or eight pesos a day.

Cam left Chimaltenango on Tuesday for the next area he was to cover as a colporteur. It was to the town of Santiago Zacatepecar. After several fruitless attempts to secure a carrier who would take his seventy-five pound load the eighteen miles, Cam proceeded on without his belongings. Cam's friends assured him they could find a carrier for an acceptable rate who would get his belongings to him on the following morning.

For the first three miles of his journey, Cam was accompanied by a baker and a carpenter. They talked together of their mutual love for the Lord and of the joy they found in serving Him. All agreed they looked forward to the day when Christ would once again come to earth. Then before sending Cam on alone, the three men stepped off the roadside into an orchard and held a short prayer meeting.

The road to Santiago was lined with trees, flowering bushes, a winding mountain stream and adobe houses freshly whitewashed in readiness to celebrate the president's birthday. Cam later learned the whitewashing was a mandatory requirement by the central government. Residents who neglected this important beautification were fined.

With his valise filled with tracts, a milk bottle filled with beans and his body conditioned like a well-tuned instrument, Cam joyfully passed out tracts to all he met on the road to Santiago. The *Mozos* or carriers he met along the way were also filled with mirth – mirth at seeing an American carrying his own load. This was of little concern to Cam, of course. He simply carried on as if everything was perfectly normal.

In the early afternoon, Cam rested by a pretty mountain stream and ate his lunch of cold black beans. At about four o'clock in the afternoon, he reached the town of Santiago only to be told that the house of his next contact, *Don* Goyo Arroyo, was still two to three miles further on. Cam rested for an hour, then tried to find a guide to help him find *Don* Goyo's house, but no one would help him.

The sun was beginning to set when Cam started out alone for *Don* Goyo's home, a rather large ranch set among the surrounding hillsides. Cam had a general idea of where he was going and what trail to take, but when he came to a junction where trails converged, he was bewildered.

In spite of the ghostly fireflies that kept me company in the bushes along the trail, I felt I was getting along quite well until I came to a place where several trails met. Unfortunately, I chose the wrong one and had to return. I then made another ill choice and would have continued in my error had I not met a couple of *mozos* who, when I asked directions, corrected me. The fireflies continued to give me a queer sensation up and down my spine, and as I was getting nearer to the place where I had made my wrong trail choice, I ran into a bunch of drunks. One of them carried a shotgun and when he spotted me, stepped up in front of me and demanded to know where I was going. I simply stepped to one side and without a word continued on my way. A few feet up the main trail, I noticed a smaller trail and turned off. At that moment the man fired his shot-gun. I presumed it was at me, but I didn't feel anything and hurried on my way.

After a long walk on this narrower trail, I came to a small hut. When I inquired about *Don* Goyo, I was relieved to find I had stumbled onto one of his neighbors. Graciously he guided me across a ravine and safely to my destination.

> Emotionally and physically spent after his long ordeal, Cam wanted nothing more than a good meal and a warm bed.

Don Goyo's wife was the motherly type and with two teenage boys of her own, knew how to keep a splendid house and prepare an equally splendid meal, which I ate with great delight.

> The meal over, Cam now faced the question of a warm bed. One of his principal laments during his many overnights in these mountain homes was lack of blankets. He truly did feel the cold and was most often most miserable.

> Now as he faced another night, Cam observed the ranch was at an altitude of 7,000 feet, built out in the open away from anything that would cut the frigid mountain air. He later wrote:

Thank goodness this house is an exception to the rule. They gave me *two* blankets! However, I soon discovered this wasn't enough to protect me from the cold. Even though I slept with all my clothes on, the only side that was warm was next to the boards.

William Cameron (Cam) Townsend (above) and Elbert (Robbie) Robinson (right) leaving for Guatemala, Fall, 1916

The Townsend Family
Back row, left to right: Ethel, Paul, Cam, Oney
Front Row: Mary, Will, Mollie, Lula

The Presbyterian American Hospital after the
Christmas Day, 1917 earthquake

*Cam's friend and companion, Francisco (Frisco)
Diaz with his wife*

*Cam and Elvira Malstrom a week after announcing
engagement - February 22, 1919*

Cam and Elvira's cornstalk house in San Antonio

Cam and Elvira in Cakchiquel dress

— 9 —

GOD WILL SEE YOU THROUGH

In readiness for their upcoming Thanksgiving conference in Guatemala City, Robbie left his responsibility in the town of Tecpan in the highlands and met Cam at the Goyo Ranch. It was a sixty-five mile ride through forests of oak and fir, and beautiful farms and gardens that looked like a giant patchwork quilt of different shades of green. Cam was overjoyed to be reunited with his traveling companion. Robbie, too, expressed his enthusiasm at seeing his colleague again. But what astonished Robbie more than all the exciting tales Cam wanted to share, was the way Cam looked. Said Robbie:

"Cam, you know Mr. Bishop and others at the mission thought you were so pale and skinny when you first arrived that you wouldn't last two months out on those hard trails. Now look at you! I have never seen anyone develop as fast as you have in just over a month. This experience is really much more valuable than two years at college. Praise God for what He has done! " Cam's response was: "The young lions do lack and suffer hunger, but they that wait upon the Lord shall not want any good thing."

To celebrate this reunion, Cam decided to make a batch of peanut brittle – even though he didn't have the peanuts. With a nickel's worth of sugar, he tried out his culinary art. It was a disaster. Cam neglected to grease the plate and in his effort to dislodge the candy, the plate broke. However, he secured some tiny seeds and made them into a candy that he said tasted like popcorn balls.

Cam and Robbie spent the next several days working out from the Goyo Ranch. Two nearby towns for which Cam felt a strange affinity were San Juan and its neighbor San Pedro. Cam recorded that San Juan was a beautiful city of ten thousand people with no resident believers. He then commented that if it was the Lord's plan for him, he would like to give his life for these two towns. "It would make a wonderful field of service for any missionary," he said.

On Saturday, November 24, the two colporteurs took turns riding Robbie's horse on the way to Guatemala City. *Don* Goyo, concerned with the appearance of one American riding while the other walked, offered to loan Cam a riding pony. Cam thanked him, but declined, and assured him that it was perfectly acceptable for an American to walk while his companion rode.

The long journey back to the city was quite different than it was the first time they had taken this road. Then the road had been full of mud. Now they were in the middle of the dry season, and the mud had turned to billows of choking dust that grew thicker and thicker the closer they came to the city. Both Cam and Robbie commented on how they would rather be back in the clean healthful air of the mountains.

While the two men longed for the uncorrupted air of their mountain regions, they were nonetheless happy to be once again in community with those who shared their ideals. As he had done in Antigua, Mr. Bishop was there to welcome the men with a special dinner and mail from home.

There were three letters waiting for me – two dandies from home and one from Mr. Smith. The one from Mr. Smith contained a forty-dollar check for both myself and Robbie. It seems that ever since Mr. Smith learned that we had to buy our tickets out of our first four-month's allowances, he had been praying that it might somehow be refunded to us. What a surprise! This has come at just the right time as both of us are rather low in funds.

They told us that there have been nearly one hundred earthquakes in various towns around the city and in some parts of the city. All of the quakes came when I was either walking or sleeping. It's strange that I didn't awaken.

The annual missions conference of the Central American Mission began on Sunday, November 25. Present were representatives from three Central American countries and six different mission societies. The meetings (mornings and afternoons) were held in the Presbyterian School for Girls, where many of the delegates roomed and boarded. Cam himself was one who had moved there for the conference.

Cam wrote that it was great to listen to and hear what the old "war horses" had to say. He was impressed with those who had pioneer experience and opened up "closed doors" to the gospel.

Some of the delegates had more than twenty years

experience and had pushed into countries where the
gospel was hated and its ministers threatened with
death. Some of the missionaries had gone barefooted.
All had traveled through mud and dust, and beneath
the hot, tropical sun and heavy rains. And after their
long journeys, they had found no comfortable home
waiting for them. They lived in small adobe houses with
beds made of pine boards. In the early days, food was
scarce, missionaries were often boycotted, and all
around were bitter enemies – people who knew nothing
of the love of Christ.

However, during this past decade the work has
grown. There are now at the time of this conference
about forty missionaries in Guatemala and nearly the
same number scattered over the other four republics of
Central America.

> Cam recorded that much of the success of the
> work was due to the advance work of the British
> and Foreign Bible Society and the work of their
> colporteurs.

> Other impressions of the conference included a
> special report from a missionary woman from Hon-
> duras who spoke on the second coming. Other mis-
> sionaries voiced their deep convictions about how
> they felt evangelism and mission work ought to be
> carried out. "All this," wrote Cam, "was carried
> out in love and without bitterness. Throughout
> there was a special sense of the unity of the Spi-
> rit."

November 26, 1917. This morning there were four
or five of us at the breakfast table. Afterward we had a
time of worship together. Something happened today
that has made me wonder why people show their pri-
vate emotions in public. Several times during this conference (I am writing this four days late), I have found

that the heart rules the head and often acts altogether without taking the head into consultation. While I was praying this morning, I mentioned "home" and my voice broke. I wasn't homesick, but I couldn't get control of my voice, no matter how hard I tried. It was like when I said good-bye in the station in Los Angeles. The train was just beginning to move, and I wanted to run and catch it, but my legs refused to move.

This same thing happened at Thanksgiving. The dinner was over and everyone was just praising God that we were here doing His work, but still many of the people – people I felt were stronghearted – had tears in their eyes. When they talked about home, the tears just came unbidden.

> The conference was notable for more than the sudden realization that Cam (and others) had feelings and emotions that needed to be expressed and to do so wasn't a sign of weakness. Cam made a note in his journal that he wanted to be sure and remember a special motto, namely: "God planned it, Jesus did it, the Spirit said it, I believed it, and that settles it." Another motto he always tried to put into practice was, "Let go and let God."

Principle of God seeing you through.
> The modern sophisticate might easily interpret such truism as a naive cliché, wholly unsuited to meet the complex structure of today's high-tech world. Mr. Townsend's life, of course, revealed that he didn't live a "formula" life. What his life did reveal was that he knew God in an intimate way and that he lived and acted upon the principle, "If God has called you, God will see you through," no matter what the odds to the contrary. If God said it, that settled it; there was no debate, and he looked to God to supply the resources, wisdom and

skill to complete the task.

Immediately after recording this important principle, Cam detailed the events surrounding the Thanksgiving dinner.

We didn't have pumpkin pie nor turkey, but there were a lot of other great things. I went easy on the solids. But when it came to cake and ice cream, I smiled at the waitress and as a result had three dishes of ice cream and seven slices of cake.

When the conference ended, Robbie decided he would remain in Guatemala City. Both men concluded that it was much in need of the gospel.

Cam on the other hand, took the train and headed south toward the port of San José. He was interested in working the plantations along the coast. Cam's plan was to travel to the coast in two states. His first stop would be fifty-eight miles by train to the town of Escuintla, a rich area noted for its abundance of tropical fruit.

In the company of two women missionaries, Cam took the second-class train toward the coast. Second-class was not only cheaper, but afforded him more people to "preach to" while he traveled.

There were two major problems with this trip. First, Cam miscalculated the number of people who were traveling and didn't have nearly enough tracts to go around. The second problem had to do with some pumpkin seed candy he bought when the train stopped at Lake Amatitlan. It gave him a severe case of dysentery that bothered him for three weeks. There was a great deal more that was to bother Cam during the weeks he trekked through the jungles. The most immediate discomfort after the boiling sun, was the multitude of biting insects.

Tuesday, December 4. I wage continual warfare. On one occasion when I was walking through the dense brush and undergrowth, hundreds of tropical ticks attached themselves to me. I was in complete misery until I found a banana plantation and secluded myself among the bananas, stripped and spent almost an hour picking off the diminutive ticks. I often marvel at the long list of sufferings the Apostle Paul endured. But I think the workers along the coast have one up on him. Here there are myriads of mosquitoes, ants and insects of all kinds. For the last two days I have been one mass of bites and will be until I leave the coast.

While he suffered the effects of these unwelcome visitors, Cam was still being troubled with dysentery. He was introduced to the medicinal effects of papaya to aid him with his problem.

A railroad man told me that papayas are good for the stomach. In fact, he said they would digest my suspender buttons. It was my first encounter with this new kind of fruit. They are about the size of a good-sized oblong muskmelon and taste halfway between a melon and a pumpkin (I'm great on the halfways!). I think I'll have to get used to the taste.

Cam's next encounter with a papaya came several days later.

Saturday, December 8. Before breakfast I helped a farmer pick his papayas. The farmer took a long pole (the trees are about twenty-feet high) to knock off the fruit while I stood at the trunk to catch it when it fell. Unfortunately the farmer missed the ripe one that I was watching and knocked off a green one that I couldn't see because of a banana leaf. The green one fell and hit me square in the eye – my first experience in picking tropical fruit. It weighed about two pounds!

Cam's acceptance among the people of the jungle plantations was often different than it had been in the highlands. Most people here, he recorded, gave him their polite attention. At one railway station the station agent (after hearing what Cam had to say) allowed him to hang his hammock in the station and treated him to a good supper and breakfast.

Later, at one large *finca*, Cam was given yet another surprise.

About two o'clock I found a good-sized plantation where I was told I would find a Swiss administrator who could speak English. His wife, a native, came to the door, and while I was presenting the gospel, her husband spoke up from the bed. He was sick with a high fever. I explained the gospel but he couldn't see the light. When I left, he gave me twenty pesos. One of the old *mozos* was also down with a fever. I couldn't make much known to him; he was nearly deaf and couldn't read.

Cam decided to leave the coastal area a few days earlier than expected and make his way back to the city of Escuintla where he would meet Robbie, Mr. Bishop and others for yet another conference. His plan was to go by way of the old port town of Iztapa. The most accessible route to this rustic village was via the Chiquimula Canal in a dugout canoe.

Sunday, December 9. There is a canal or lagoon leading along the coast from San José to Iztapa and they say nearly to El Salvador. I hadn't expected to leave San José until Monday, but it was impossible to get passage except at two p.m. and midnight today, and as there was no adequate accommodation, I decided to take the one at two o'clock. After saying good-bye to the folks on the train, I hustled about and was able to visit most of the stores and houses before leaving. By the way, there is a Chinese man in San José who makes real American pies.

I was able to secure passage in the first canoe leaving which carried the first marimba that Iztapa could call its own. Four young fellows of the town had bought it and were preparing to make their first appearance in public during the Christmas festivals. The men were proud of their fine big instrument. The canoe was hewn out of a large log about twenty feet in length by three feet in width. The man with the pole stood at the stern. At first we floated in what was nothing more than a shallow ditch. But as soon as the incoming tide filled the canal, we were off. At last we came to broad lagoons with great mangrove trees jungled on either side. The limbs sent down roots even from a height of thirty feet. As a result, the trees looked as though many vines were hanging from them. There were numerous fish, and the jungle seems alive with egrets and herons, not to mention the bunches of brilliant butterflies. At one place we saw an alligator basking in the sun. There was a peculiar sweet, sickening smell rising from the water.

We made the nine miles in two and a half hours. Iztapa lies alongside a river and this has formed a bar which we had to cross before reaching the town. Along in the eighties, when Rufino Barrios was president, they planned to make a port of Iztapa. Wharves were constructed and a railway was built joining the mainline at Obrero. When Barrios was killed, the project was dropped. Now the wharves are nearly covered by sand washed up by the river and the railway is nearly lost in the undergrowth of the jungle. The town is open to the sea breeze and is cooler and more healthy than further inland. The two hundred inhabitants are quite prosperous as nature has blessed the place with natural resources aplenty. The lands are rich and produce fine rice and two splendid crops of corn. I thought since Iztapa was such an out-of-the-way place the chances were good for me to plant the seeds of the gospel in virgin soil.

Principle of pioneering and Romans 15:20.

From the inception of WBT and SIL, Mr. Townsend believed the primary goal of every translator was evangelization through the translated New Testament Scriptures. The overpowering motivation for this thrust was that if Christ had not already returned when every tribe and nation had been evangelized, He would then return. For this reason, Romans 15:20 became a central key to his mission - almost a rallying cry: "Yes, so have I strived to preach the gospel, not where Christ was named, lest I should build upon another man's foundation."

Esther Matteson, co-translator of the Piro New Testament, once asked Uncle Cam to assign two more SIL people to the Piros. It was a legitimate request. Esther wanted to establish an institute to train and prepare Piro Christian young people for the gospel ministry. Cam's response reflected his strong belief in pioneering and his conviction that Bible translation would hasten the day of Christ's return. "Esther," said Cam, "If we do that for every tribe, when will we get through? When are we going to reach the more than two thousand who do not have any Scripture in their language? We must pioneer." Esther countered with how deeply she felt about the Piro young peoples' need for a training school; to which Cam replied, "Esther, we must stick to pioneering. Let's pray that God will raise up someone else to assume this responsibility." In tears, both Uncle Cam and Esther prayed for God to lay it upon the heart of another to assume this important work. Within six months God had answered that prayer. The Swiss Indian Mission assigned, in Cam's words, "the most talented and best prepared man he had yet met to establish such a training school."

After we emerged from the mangrove lagoon and landed on the sand dunes, we came upon a large clearing where lay the town of Iztapa. Immediately after landing, I called on the military headquarters and presented my passport. Afterward I located a *posada* [a place to eat and sleep].

It was a particular joy for me to present the gospel to the people of Iztapa, most of whom have never heard the gospel story.

Most were sympathetic as long as I told them only about Christ's dying to save them from the penalty of sin. But when I told them of how He saves from sin itself, they no longer cared to listen. With a few exceptions, they love the wickedness of their old hearts too much to want it taken out.

Cam's first night in Iztapa was interrupted by great hordes of mosquitoes that stung him with such a vengeance he was forced to move from his sleeping hammock to a bed in another hut. This served two positive purposes. It gave him relief from the mosquitoes and also from a group of men who had been sitting around his hammock talking and drinking.

The next morning Cam decided to follow an abandoned railway track through the jungle to the main line and the town of El Tigre. A young man he met the night before promised to be his guide.

Monday, December 10. Following the old track was

hard work. The track was poorly marked and in some places completely overgrown with thick jungle. In other places the swamp had undermined the tracks and it was difficult, almost impossible, to tell which way they went. I am told this route is impossible in the rainy season. I believe it. There is no evidence that anyone has passed this way since the last rainy season.

Forcing your way through thick undergrowth with a thirty-pound pack, wading swamps, fighting off mosquitoes in hot, sticky weather is difficult at the best of times. But it is doubly hard on one with dysentery!

Finally after a full day of difficult travel, I arrived within two miles of the *finca* and found a good road. Happily I hit upon five ox teams coming out of the jungle. They had been hauling cedar logs, the ones from which cigar boxes are made. I climbed onto one of them and rode the rest of the way to the *finca*.

The owner of the *finca* received me cordially. These plantation owners are always glad to see a traveler, provided he is of correct social standing. Then, as he did for me, they break out their best food. In this case, it was a fine meal of fried rice, beans, tortillas, cheese and coffee, a much finer meal than this poor colporteur had had for many days.

I forgot to mention that before eating, I was given the privilege of taking a shower bath. It served two purposes: one of getting rid of all the day's grime and sweat, and two, freeing me of the tiny ticks that had attached themselves to me during the long trek through the jungle.

After a good night's rest and a fine breakfast, it was an easy walk to the main train line. From there I took the train for Escuintla and arrived just in time to meet Robbie and Mr. Bishop who had arrived from Guatemala City.

— 10 —

EARTHQUAKE

True to his word, Francisco Díaz (Frisco), Cam's new friend whom he had met in the highlands, arrived in Escuintla in mid-December with the pastor from Antigua, *Don* Isidro. Cam noted that Frisco came with his hair cut, a new pair of sandals and a broad smile. He then recorded that it was a great blessing to have his new friend along since now they could evangelize in the Cakchiquel language. Cam was becoming increasingly aware that he was not communicating in Spanish with the many Indian people he was meeting. Also, as he and Frisco traveled throughout the coastal plantations from December 15-23, Cam began to chafe under a social inequity that presented him with great misgivings. It was the unjust and dehumanizing practice of indentured labor.

With each plantation visit, I am made painfully aware of the plight of the indentured Indian. I have found thousands of highland-born Indian people who are now entrapped by the *colono* system. This system is virtual slavery. They have been brought to live and work year-round on the coastal plantations. The Indian borrows a small amount of money from the landowner, generally for the purpose of drinking. If he cannot pay

back his debt, the Indian is forced by the government
to serve the lender for a certain length of time each
year at a small wage. Unfortunately, the Indian never
seems to be able to pay off his debt. If the plantation
is sold, the *colono* is transferred to serve the new master. Further, a *colono* is not allowed to leave the plantation without permission.

On some of these plantations I found stocks and
whipping posts. One Indian told me of how he was
whipped until he was almost unconscious. Another told
how he was strung up by his thumbs and made to sit
for days in the stocks unsheltered from the sun. By law,
these practices are outlawed, but a landowner can still
do what he wills with any *colono* on his plantation. And
the poor Indian is so frightened, he seldom dares to
report mistreatment to the authorities. Since the Indians are brought from all over the republic to work the
plantations, there is a splendid opportunity to preach
and spread the gospel. Unlike other places, the people
on the plantations are not embittered against the gospel or the *evangélicos*.

At one plantation, seven Indians professed to accept
Christ. In yet another place, one old man was so delighted with the selected Scripture portions I gave him,
that he hugged them in his arms and danced around the
hut. Afterward he went over to a basketful of tortillas,
took out a stack and gave them to me.

On another plantation, Frisco and I had a unique experience with the richest man in the republic. It was
about midday, and we had just finished visiting a large
group of huts. We were eating our meager lunch under
the shade of the carpenter's shed when up rode the
owner of the plantation. He spoke first to Frisco and
wanted to know who I was and what we were doing on
his plantation. When he learned the nature of our
business, he told us not to bother going over to his

larger plantation where he said he had over five hundred *mozos* working.

Six months later I learned that this man bought another plantation where there was a large congregation of believers. When he discovered this, he ordered his administrator to disperse all of them. But the administrator pleaded with the owner saying that these believers were his best workers.

The owner then watched for himself, and after some time came to the same conclusion as his administator – that, indeed, the believers were the better workers. Since the owner was a practical man, he overcame his theological prejudices, and threw all his plantations open to the gospel. On some of the plantations he even provided, at his own expense, chapels where the believers could hold services.

Later, when he became president of the republic, he was willing to show kindness toward those whom he had previously considered foreign intruders. As a result of this, other plantation owners opened their doors to the gospel in the hope that their *mozos* would become converted and then become better laborers!

Even though Cam enjoyed the special hospitality he was afforded at the plantation manor houses, he decided on this trip that he and Frisco would forgo these visits. The reason was simply that it took too much time away from visiting the workers in the fields and in their huts.

Cam recorded that a simple meal of beans and tortillas often took up to an hour for the maid to prepare. And if they should be offered anything more complicated, it would require two hours or longer.

Since Cam and Frisco had a limited amount of time to work the plantations before Cam left to spend Christmas in Guatemala City, Cam decided they could make the best use of their time and cover more ground if they carried their food with them. But what kind of food would be suitable? Cam discovered the answer one morning in the market.

December 20, 1917. This morning we bought seven bottles [five bottles to the gallon] of honey for about twenty-five American cents. I put five bottles of honey in my canteen and the other two we packed in the valise for the folks back in Escuintla. After our breakfast of honey and tortillas, we hurried on to a nearby *finca*.

The first man we met was open to the message but wouldn't make a decision. In the second house we found a fanatical woman who tried to make trouble for us. But further on we met another woman who blessed us and sent us on our way with an egg and a papaya. As we passed down another row of huts, we met two Indian women whom I am quite sure of meeting in heaven. One was an old lady who for many years had been searching for spiritual truth, and under Frisco's guidance, came to know our Lord. The other was an intelligent-looking middle-aged woman who was also convinced of Frisco's message and indicated her desire to follow the Lord.

It was apparent that the Lord had given Frisco a great gift of leading people to Himself. At one plantation, he started a conversation with an Indian who had been standing around watching us talk to some of the other workers. As Frisco went deeper into his explanation, I could hear the Indian exclaim every now and then, "It's the truth; it's the truth!" For over an hour they studied the Scriptures together, and then with gladness, the Indian man accepted Christ.

We are nearly out of tracts now and in order to get

back to Guatemala City at our appointed time, we are being forced to bypass some of the out-of-the-way towns. In all probability, these places will not hear the gospel for months, perhaps years, and this burdens me. Nevertheless, we began our nine-mile walk through the tropical forest to the town of Ziquinila. When we came within two miles of this town, we happened upon a good-sized *finca* and here Frisco led two more Indians to the Lord. A fine-looking middle-aged man and his wife had been prepared by the Lord for our visit. When Frisco presented the message and then asked if they wanted to confess Christ as Lord, the woman, a slight little thing, stepped forward, and with folded hands and an earnest, trusting look in her eyes, looking up to heaven said, "I accept Jesus as my Lord and Savior."

We left these two Indian people and walked about another half-mile and came to the edge of a large banana grove. Just behind this and topped by the more distant volcano, Fuego, lay the hill of Ziquinila. It had a table-like peak at each end with a saddle in between. This view, coupled with giant tropical trees dotted here and there and a clear stream of running water, made an ideal place to camp.

After gaining permission from the administrator of the banana grove *finca*, we swung our hammocks from a post to a banana stalk. However, it proved to be too weak and I made my bed on the ground. After a supper of tortillas and honey, we laid down under the light of the moon rejoicing that the insects were absent.

Saturday, December 22. We had trouble getting tortillas this morning. People told us that corn is very high-priced. Frisco finally bought a few in a hut that wasn't too far from where we had slept. We just poured the honey on a little thicker! Francisco had brought along some toasted tortillas that he calls *toto posti*. We topped off our breakfast with these.

Between our camp and the town, we stopped at a *finca* and were treated to a coconut. Ziquinila is a town of small orchards. Every house had a number of mango, chico and zapote fruit trees. Despite the location of this town in the excessive heat belt, it's rather pleasant because of the shade cast by the many fruit trees. Happily, it is also free of insects.

Since the town is off the main railway line and there are just a few cart trails, commerce is slow here. However, the people seem self-satisfied and display a quiet attentive attitude. The mayor and the *comandante* listened to the message most attentively. We found only one family who had ever heard the gospel, but they were not ready to accept the Lord.

When I knocked on the door of another house, the man said he had heard of the gospel before, and then threw open the door and said, "Come in and sit down. I want to hear all about this matter." We talked for nearly an hour, after which his wife served us orangeade.

At noon I was extravagant and paid twenty-five cents for a meal at a better home. When I asked about the trail back to Escuintla, everyone laughed. They all said that it was so bad that hardly anyone ever took it.

About three o'clock we left the town of Ziquinila and headed for Escuintla (from there I was to take the tram back to the capital) with the hope of sleeping at a *finca* along the way. Almost immediately the trail became rocky and for five miles led us among *fincas* that were more or less run-down.

About five o'clock we began to worry about tortillas, to the extent that although the next hut we found was about as dirty as anything I ever saw, we bought two and a half cents worth of cold tortillas – all they had to spare.

We had two or three rivers to cross where I had to

take off my shoes. Just before dark we sat down on a bluff overlooking a river and ate our tortillas and honey. A passerby told us it was only three miles to the next *finca*, so we decided to try to reach it before making camp. It was now getting quite dark, and the way was rough and hard to follow. To add color to the experience, it began to rain. The drops seemed to be as big as grapes. In a few minutes we were soaking wet. As we came out of the last pasture, we saw a light ahead and started to run toward it. But to our dismay, we found another river between us and the light. I took off my shoes and rolled up my pants, and we were successful in getting across without going above our knees. Finding our way by flashlight, we hurried on to the hacienda where we found the owner of what proved to be a large *finca*. He was rather cold at first, thinking the sky was raining Germans, but when he learned I was an American, he made us quite at home. We hung our hammocks on the porch, and although he and his wife were sitting on the porch reading, I couldn't wait for them to retire. I stripped off my wet clothes, wrapped up in my blanket and went to sleep.

Sunday, December 23. They told us that there wasn't another house in the remaining twelve miles to Escuintla. Accordingly, we breakfasted before leaving. It took about an hour and a half to visit all the huts. There were few who could read, but these few were well occupied when we left them reading material.

The trail was shaded most of the way by giant trees. My spirit ran high, and as my legs tried to set a similar pace, Frisco had to break into a trot every little while. After crossing a shallow river, we sat down on some boulders and held a little prayer and Bible study service. At one place we surprised a young deer that quickly bolted through the underbrush.

We arrived in Escuintla before noon. Some believers

prepared a fine meal for us, after which we bathed in a creek and changed our clothes. I left Frisco, who was to go overland to Antigua and bring his family to the capital while I took the afternoon train arriving at the mission building about seven o'clock.

Monday, December 24. I found that Robbie was still living in the Presbyterian School for Girls, but as it was so far away and for so short a time, I didn't go over to sleep. Two letters from home were waiting for me. Before I could get away in the afternoon, the young ladies put me to work on the Christmas tree which I finished barely in time to look after my passport.

> With his time divided between helping trim a Christmas tree, buying a few Christmas presents and getting his passport renewed, Cam was unable to write one of his lengthy letters to the "home folks." He did, however, manage to scribble off a postcard.

Guatemala City
December 24, 1917

Dear Home Folks,

Just got back from Escuintla Sunday night, late. Yesterday I had to help out on a Christmas tree, then renew my passport. This morning two of the young men who will be working under me came in from a city forty-eight miles out. I have given the morning to them, helping one man's wife get a job. I am now on my way to Christmas dinner at the Bishops, and since the mail goes out at five o'clock, I am sending only this card.

Had a wonderful trip last week. Traveled fifty miles on foot through as beautiful scenery as I have ever seen. Worked twenty different *fincas;* one had a population of three thousand. One day Frisco had five people come to know the Lord. He is great. I was able to lead two Ladinos to the Lord. Slept in the fields two nights.

Lived on honey and tortillas for eight meals. Honey was only eighteen cents a gallon. I carried it in my canteen so we always had a meal if we couldn't find anything else. I am in the pink of condition except for a myriad of wood tick bites and other insects. Haven't had a chance to write in my diary. Many thanks for writing to me.

Lovingly,
Cameron

Christmas was a day filled with happy, relaxed fellowship, a great dinner with the Bishops, the arrival of the two young men who would be helping Cam, and excitement about the next phase in Cam's itinerary as a colporteur. It had been agreed, in consultation with Mr. Bishop, that Cam would leave immediately after Christmas and spend six weeks in El Salvador. From there he would go on to Honduras.

During the day, Cam's plans changed several times. Some friends were leaving early the next morning for Honduras and Cam wanted to be up early to bid them farewell. Since these friends were staying near the Presbyterian Girls' School, Cam decided to visit Robbie and spend the night at the school rather than at the mission building, provided there were blankets for him.

Tired after a long, full day, Cam retired early. He almost never woke from his sleep. His letter dated January 1, 1918 explained why in graphic detail.

Guatemala City
January 1, 1918

Dear Home Folks,

Since I wrote my card, things have been terribly upset here. I was staying with Robbie at the Presbyterian school and was in bed and asleep by 9:30. Before going to bed, I felt some pretty strong quakes but since the earth had been quaking on and off for the last two months, no one had been paying attention to it. In fact, some of the fellows had been making little jokes about how they weren't afraid of the quakes.

Robbie retired about ten o'clock and was just dozing off to sleep at 10:30 when there was a tremendous jolt, and he jumped toward the door. At the door, he looked back and saw me sleeping, and at the risk of his life, returned to arouse me. I didn't realize what he was talking about until I put up my hand by my head and felt a large chunk of plaster. Immediately, I pulled on my trousers and shoes and ran downstairs. I wanted to finish my night's rest, so took my bedding with me. As I went out the door, I grabbed a stack of laundry which I thought would serve as a pillow. The servants were all down in the patio preparing to spend the night, but the quakes kept coming. People in the community were coming out of their houses to warn the authorities to turn off the electricity.

Rob and I decided to go out into the street to see what damage had been done. The hospital is just back of the school, and we found nurses with their patients in a vacant lot across from the building, trying to keep everyone warm.

The Aberles, a missionary couple who lived near the school and were planning to leave for Honduras in the morning, came over to see if they could help anyone, but when the quaked continued, they decided to go home, and Rob and I started with them. Just as we got around the corner of the school, the quakes became stronger and the Aberles began to run. Rob and I started back toward the hospital, but had no sooner gotten out into the open, when the whole earth started to roll and rock. Tiles from rooftops fell and walls caved in. As soon as it was over, Rob and I decided to cross the city to see if everyone in the mission building was safe. By now it was about 10:45.

Just as we rounded the corner of the hospital, there came a dramatic jolt. It was the jolt that was to do the most damage. The earth seemed to rise right up in front of us and hang there quivering. Walls swayed back and forth until they could stand it no longer. The school building, a fine brick building, stood the shock except for the cornices and part of the brick wall. In the moonlight, the hospital appeared to be totally ruined. But in the morning when we could examine it more closely, we discovered only the second story was destroyed.

As we hurried toward the mission, we struggled to get through the streets that were full of debris and people screaming and fleeing from their houses. The quakes were now coming every few minutes. We kept on the run, dodging from buildings we thought might fall on us.

When we came to the center of town where the Allisons lived, we found the streets leading to their home completely filled with debris and tangled wire. We made our way through and found them still in the house. The upper story was made of wood, so they thought it safer than being in the street. The church and the printing plant were badly damaged by the heavy cornices that had fallen.

We were going on to the Central American Mission when we thought about the people in the orphans' home and started toward them. As we walked along, we saw people huddled about in the streets trying to keep warm. A great many had rescued their saints and were calling upon them and singing "Ave Marías." As we neared the penitentiary, the earth began to roll, almost like the sea. We wondered if the ground wouldn't open up. The big penitentiary walls, two and a half feet thick, had fallen.

When we arrived at the orphanage, we found the women who were responsible for the children had gotten them out safely, but the school building was ruined. From there we went to the mission building. It was a three-story brick building, and we fully expected our little rooms on the upper story to have fallen, but the building was still standing, though badly damaged, and everyone had gotten out safely. I later learned from the Bishops that the building would have to be completely rebuilt.

Right near the mission four men lay dead. They had been killed in a poorly-built hotel. Soldiers were beginning to take charge of affairs, but most were drinking a good bit to keep up their courage.

By now we were getting pretty cold, and I decided to cross town and see if any of the laundry I had rescued was wearable. The Allisons were still in the house and told us to come in, too. We told them we would return after seeing if the Aberles were all right, and we had gotten some clothes.

We found that the Aberles and some of the other missionaries were safe. After telling them of the news of the city, we went to the hospital. The laundry happened to contain two suits of underwear and socks, so we dressed a little warmer.

The patients and nurses were quite cold as they were sleeping on the ground. The nurses asked Rob to go up to the second floor of the school and bring down some blankets, but since the quakes were still coming every few minutes, I advised him not to go. However, Rob went, but had no more than entered the building, when there came another tremendous jolt, and he returned. I think the ladies joshed him about coming back because pretty soon he again went over to the building. In a few minutes another quake came and I ran over to see if he had gone inside. However, he had just started up the stairs when the quake came, and for the second time, he returned. We decided it was better for the ladies to suffer a little cold than to risk our lives in the building. But when we saw that they were really shivering with cold, we mustered up our courage and decided to make the attempt together. We did so on the run. We raced up the stairs and sped around the corridors at the same breakneck speed, found the blankets and returned before another quake.

After this "heroism" we went back to the Allisons, and despite the shaking earth, got about an hour's sleep before six o'clock. After a little breakfast I went to help at the hospital, and Rob went to the orphanage.

The city was in ruins, although there were a few houses that had only minor damage. I constructed a little tent out of sheets and blankets and then went over to the Central American Mission and changed my clothes. Next, I called on the Minister of War, who had taken his post in the central plaza, to see if I could be of any service in getting food to the city. He was quite interested and told his general to take me to see the man who had charge of the city's food supplies. While we waited for a few moments, I spoke to the major about closing the saloons as some of the saloon keepers were selling liquor in the streets. The major said this was a good suggestion and he would give the orders to the general who was to have accompanied me. Except for the first time when there was quite a bit of drinking, the order to close the saloons was well-enforced.

— 11 —

GOD, A VERY PRESENT HELP IN TROUBLE

Cam's first three months in Guatemala followed no well-constructed plan. His day-to-day events unfolded and interconnected in such an unexpected way that an observer would have asked, "What's going to happen next?" Until the Christmas Day earthquake that almost leveled Guatemala City, Cam's plans were to proceed southeast to the town of Barberena and then into El Salvador. But now all that had changed.

Following that long night of terror when the earth refused to be still, Cam assisted Robbie at the orphanage. In his detailed letter to his parents written January 1, 1918, Cam explained the nature of his task and what happened during those terrible days and nights.

Rob and I had to move a great deal of furniture into the yard of the orphanage. It kept us busy all Wednesday afternoon and into Thursday moving the furniture over to a field where the Butler family is now located. The first night there were so many drunks around that we decided to guard the furniture. I stood guard for the first part of the night and Rob the second. Out of the past forty-two hours, I have slept only two. However, Rob fared worse than I. The frequency of the aftershocks prevented him from sleeping.

By Friday of that week, conditions in the city had deteriorated to near-famine levels. What food remained was greatly inflated. One government official requested that the missions become an agent of the government and take charge of food distribution, including the food that would come from the United States. As much as they wanted to help, the missions, after a hastily-convened meeting, felt this was too large a job for them to handle. Because they needed food for themselves and the poor believers, Cam was the one commissioned to go to Antigua to purchase two or three tons of corn and beans. After he had been given an official letter by the authorities giving him permission to bring food into the city, Cam left about five o'clock on Friday afternoon.

My plan was to travel the first fifteen miles to the home of an Indian believer who was also a worker in the mission. About eight miles out, I passed through the town of Mixco. It was in ruins, but on the outskirts, in a radius of a mile or so, none of the houses were down. It was getting dark, and I lost my way trying to find the believer's little ranch and didn't arrive until nine o'clock. I reached Antigua early the next morning, and with some difficulty, succeeded in securing about three tons of corn and beans plus two carloads of firewood. Many people in Antigua are sleeping outside, just as they are in the capital.

On Saturday afternoon about two o'clock, while I was in Antigua, the capital experienced another hard jolt. This killed about five hundred people.

After a seventy-five mile ride, I arrived back in the capital late Monday night. All along the trail I met long processions of men, women and children doing penance.

Everyone was carrying a stone up the long hill from Antigua. All were calling upon the saints to stop the earthquakes. I also met hundreds of people flocking out of the capital.

The government seems to have things well in hand now. Food is being distributed freely, and order is being preserved. However, the cemetery presents another serious problem. Many of the coffins have been shaken out of their elegant mausoleums, exposing the corpses. There is the fear that disease might spread throughout the city; therefore, all the bodies are being collected and burned. I am afraid this has had an effect on me. For many nights after I saw this, I could see nothing in my dreams but cold, stiff mummies with their toes pointed heavenward.

About seventy-five percent of the homes and buildings in the city have been destroyed. People who could not flee the city have begun to construct little sheds – corrugated iron, boards, tiles – anything that can be salvaged from the crumbled buildings is being used to put up temporary shelters. Carpenters' wages have doubled. The American Red Cross has donated a large sum of money for relief work and a corps of workers is erecting a tent city where many are finding refuge. It makes me feel proud of the U.S.A.

Shelters have been made, the corn and beans given out and medical help has been provided. Many of the believers have given splendid testimony to their living faith. One old mother, as whe watched her home crumble about her, smiled and said, "It doesn't matter; I have an eternal mansion prepared for me in heaven."

Psalm 46:1,2 has become a great source of comfort and strength to many. "God is our refuge and strength, a very present help in trouble. Therefore will not we fear, though the earth be removed, and though the mountains be carried into the midst of the sea." And

verse ten: "Be still and know that I am God; I will be
exalted among the heathen; I will be exalted in the
earth." All of these verses seem to have been written
especially for these earthquake times.

And God has indeed been exalted. Meetings have
been held in the open, tracts distributed, and all over
the republic, people are more ready to listen to the gospel. (Although some of the more fanatical people insist
that the catastrophe was God's judgment upon the
country for not driving out the *evangélicos*.)

> In the days that followed, Cam and Robbie found
> their own temporary earthquake shelter with the
> Butlers. According to Cam, the tiny shelter accom-
> modated ten people.

Mother and father have their bed in the room that
serves the triple purpose of kitchen, dining room and
parlor. Above the bed swings a hammock in which two
of the children sleep. To be sure there are inconven-
iences, but these are great days.

The house is across a ravine from the main part of the
city and has a pretty grove of cypress trees around it.
This protects it from the dust and turmoil which is so
great everywhere else.

**Principle of always being open to being used (for a tes-
timony and for practical help to others).**

> Mr. Townsend's response to the aftermath of the
> earthquake reveals, as does an examination of his
> whole life, that he wasn't in the least self-conscious
> about who he was or his limitations. He knew him-
> self to be a child of God, an instrument to be used
> by God in extending God's kingdom upon earth, in
> whatever circumstance of life he found himself.
> He never doubted that God could, and would use
> him if he were willing and open, no matter how
> weak or limited he felt himself to be.

In an interesting way, Cam was a man who didn't seem to know that there might be limitations to his potential. Thus he was free from the illusions about his own power and was able to seek from God Himself the greater strength and persistence needed for the larger task. He believed implicitly in what the Apostle Paul said in 2 Corinthians 12:9-10: ". . . my power is made perfect in weakness . . . for when I am weak, then I am strong."

For two weeks after the earthquake, Cam neglected his usual practice of journaling. He did, however, write two letters home — one on January 15; the other on the 22nd, the day he left the capital and began his journey toward El Salvador via the town of Barberena.

In the January 15 letter, Cam assured his parents that in spite of the earthquake, the mails and packages were getting through even though the central post office was in ruins. Speaking of ruins, Cam related that except for the printing machine and the wooden part of the parsonage, everything else in the Presbyterian mission was destroyed.

Cam wrote briefly of his schedule, saying that after six weeks in El Salvador, he wanted to spend March and April in Honduras. He then told about his plans to return home July 1 after a quick trip through Mexico. He showed his enthusiasm for his future plans by telling his parents that he wanted to return to the field immediately after finishing college. Part of the letter explained his Christmas present to his father.

I am sending you the hide of a mountain cat, or tropical fox as the people here call it. I think it will be good for Papa to put his feet on when he gets in and out of

bed. However, I showed the hide to a woman missionary and she put it over her shoulder and said that it
would make a beautiful fur for my sister. The five of
you can settle the matter. I have a hard time finding
presents for men.

Cam concluded the letter by saying that he was
sorry his father wasn't feeling well, and that the
climate in Guatemala would make a boy of him
again. The surprise ending of the letter came when
Cam wrote: "Everyone here tells me I'm so fat I
look like a Kewpie doll."

In the January 22 letter, Cam explained that he
had hoped by this date to have been on his way
south to Barberena, but simply could not leave the
capital with so much work to do. He did say, however, that he was packed and ready to leave that
very afternoon with his companion Frisco.

Cam's concluding sentences were pure Townsend
and reflected two principles that he and his two
organizations have always tried to follow, namely:

**Principle of starting at the top nationally and locally,
and of finding ways to keep in touch with new and old
host country friends.**

I have bought New Testaments with the money you
sent me. One for each of the president's cabinet. In presenting these to them, we will have an opportunity to
give them the gospel.

Tuesday, January 22, 1918. Off at last for Barberena.
I turned over to Rob what little business I had in the
city (the disposal of the produce which was yet to arrive
from Antigua), and prepared to leave after dinner. It
has been nearly a month since I returned from Escuintla and I was anxious to get back on the road again.
Although the opportunities for evangelization are won-

derful now in the capital, I think they are even greater in the outlying districts. There are enough workers in the city, and since I like the country work better and am more footloose to do it, I decided to do my best to leave. I kept hustling before noon, packing and writing a letter home, and by two o'clock I had everything fixed for my departure. Rob took a picture of all the folks camped in General Lima's garden and then after a word of prayer by Mr. Bishop, we left. Rob accompanied us partway toward La Reforma. I must say Mr. Bishop and others were loathe to let Rob go. He has proved himself useful and skillful in building shelters, and in so many other ways. Mrs. Bishop also came along with the buggy just then and gave us a lift of nearly a mile. La Reforma used to be a pretty drive. It's where an exposition was held some years ago and where several public buildings were erected, but they are in ruins now, and the statues have fallen.

Climbing the range of hills about a league out from town, we fell in with a *mozo* to whom we preached the gospel as we went. About 4:30 we stopped to eat supper. The people we met were keenly interested in the gospel, but also in money. They charged us double for some poorly-cooked beans and warmed-up tortillas. It was a bright moonlit night and after supper we walked on until we came to a shed without walls about nine miles from town. Here we stopped and made camp. Frisco slept on the ground, and I slept in my hammock.

Wednesday, January 23. The night was beautiful and the moon shone like day. I had brought along both of my blankets, but about midnight I woke feeling an intense cold. The wind was blowing in such a way as to put a Santa Ana* to shame. It was driving great clouds

---

*Santa Anas are seasonal winds that blow down through the canyons of Southern California.

of fog so dense that the moon was darkened. Our wall-less hut gave us little shelter. I rolled up in my blankets a little tighter and manager to get off to sleep. About three o'clock I awakened again. My hammock was swinging like a cradle, but the cold kept me from sleeping. Frisco looked comfortable on the ground, so I took down my hammock and made a bed beside him.

After shivering through a cold breakfast, we spent an hour in a sheltered place studying the Word. Our breakfast had been rather slight, and so before starting on our journey again, I went across the road to a hut and succeeded in trading a Scripture portion booklet for some tortillas. Because we had spent all our small change on the meal the night before, the barter was necessary. A mile or so down the road, we succeeded in getting a twenty-five peso bill changed and as the wind had died down, we decided to work the town of Frijanes instead of hurrying on to Barberena as we had intended to do.

Before deciding definitely on this, I would skip a house now and then to make better time. I was about to pass one house when I looked up and saw a woman regarding me curiously. I went back, gave her a tract and preached the gospel. She invited us inside the gate to explain more. We did so and succeeded in exchanging a Testament for a meal of beans and tortillas. After eating, we explained the gospel further and she finally professed to believe. She then asked prayers for her husband who, she said, was an awful drunkard. She had apparently bought a great deal of medicines in an effort to cure him, but nothing worked. As we spoke to her, a drunken woman came in and warned her that she was listening to "accursed *evangélicos.*" But even this warning didn't frighten her. Before leaving, I knelt down and prayed for the woman and her husband. I asked that this new believer in Christ would remain faithful to her commitment and that her husband might also come to know the Lord Jesus Christ, and that their home might become a gospel chapel.

Two months later, Cam learned how God had heard and answered that prayer. *Don* Manuel Marroquín, a noted evangelist, was riding through the town of Frijanes one day and as he went down the road, a woman hailed him and asked if he was Marroquín, the evangelist. When *Don* Manuel assured her he was, she then invited him to her home. For a moment he hesitated, thinking that perhaps she might be playing a trick on him, but she was so insistent, he decided to go with her. When they arrived, he discovered her one-room house was decorated with pine needles and a group of people were gathered. Noticing a Bible House Underscored New Testament on the table, he asked her if she was a believer. The woman burst into tears and told him the following story:

"One night our cow strayed away and my husband, a terrible drinker, blamed me for it. In the morning, he started out to find the cow, saying as he left that if he came back without the cow, he would cut me to pieces with his machete. But I remained faithfully at home, not knowing what to do.

"About midday a foreigner and an Indian came along and explained the way of salvation. I believed, and for a meal of beans and tortillas, received this New Testament. So great was my joy that I waited for the return of my drunken husband released from all fear.

At last he returned, without the cow, but he did not carry out his threat. When he came inside he saw the New Testament and asked what it was. I explained what had happened when he was gone and suggested he attend the meetings next Sunday in Barberena, eighteen miles away, as invited by the colporteur. To my surprise, he went to the meeting, and to my still greater surprise, he returned a saved man.

So great was the change in my husband that the neighbors asked what had happened. My husband told them his own story, and some of them also believed.

When we were told that the famous evangelist *Don* Manuel Marroquín was going to pass through our town, those who have come to believe gathered in our house for a meeting."

But that wasn't the end of the story. A year later, the husband had led twenty-three people to the Lord and had become a colporteur with the Los Angeles Bible House!

Delayed for longer than they had expected in the town of Frijanes, Cam and Frisco walked three of the eighteen miles to the town of Barberena and spent the night camped on the side of a volcanic hill.

Cam's only complaint that night was that he had to move his bed "only once because of the large *sanpopos* (ants)." Otherwise, he "passed a dandy night."

After breakfast and our study hour, we started on. The road from here to Barberena is lined with volcanic rock. However, the coffee groves do well. We had slept just outside a large town called Cerro Redondo. Most of the people we met on the *fincas* were all very poor. In the place of money, they paid us in *fichas* or trading checks to be redeemed at the company store.

Two people bought Testaments but when they were threatened by a local priest, they returned them and we gave them their money back. One woman went to the trouble of gathering up a number of tracts from her neighbors and burnt them in front of Frisco who was waiting for me. He asked the blessings of God upon her. We didn't finish the town until nearly three o'clock and still had seven miles to go. There were no houses on the road for some distance, so we made good time except once when we took shelter from a short shower.

By five o'clock, we were within a league of Barberena, but since there were a number of houses, we decided to eat before entering the town. Besides beans and tortillas, we bought overripe bananas – four dozen for a nickel. I forgot to say that on the road we met some Indians who had heard of us and the gospel from some other Indians who had come over with their tracts from S. Andrea Ozuna (near Escuintla), almost seventy-five miles from where we worked the week before Christmas. They bought two Testaments and promised to attend the meetings in Barberena.

We arrived in Barberena by moonlight and were walking down the street when two soldiers came running after us and said I would have to go with them to the plaza to give my name. They told us everyone who comes from the capital must register. I was well-received by the officer in charge, left my name, and returned to the home of *Don* Cipriano where I had left Frisco with the cargo. The folks had just returned from prayer meeting. They said they had just had two earthquakes and while we were talking, we had another one. In the morning I learned that more houses had fallen in Guatemala City.

That night I swung my hammock and Frisco made his bed in a room where there were already two beds and a counter. It was small, but we all looked after our own affairs as if we had been partitioned off from one another.

January 25, 1918. After lunch, I laid down on a bench beside the door that opened on to the street. Frisco sat in the doorway, studying a tract. A soldier came along and asked him to explain what he was reading. Another came, and another, until there was quite a crowd. I woke up in time to hear one of the soldiers say, "Man, this is just what I have been wanting for a long time." I thought it best to lie still and listen. Just then *Don* Cipriano came in from the yard and started to give them a sermon. He was getting along fine when the corporal came along and said that he was going to report this meeting to his commander-in-chief. Everyone hurriedly scattered except the one I had heard speak. He stayed and received some tracts, then promised to try to get a leave of absence to attend the meetings. In the afternoon, Frisco and I worked alone and nearly finished the city. When we returned, we found a large number of people who wanted their pictures taken, but I had to say no to all except the native pastor. I took so many pictures of the ruins that I am short of film.

I like the pastor and his family very much although his wife lets the children run around with a week's dirt on their faces like all the other children. Still, she is a hard worker, had our meals on time and well-prepared, and they try to make me feel at home. The pastor is getting feeble and seems to be rather discouraged, mainly because of finances. As pastor, he is supposed to evangelize and look after the work of an area half as large as Los Angeles County. He has a family of six that he has to support on $12.50 U.S. per month. In order to evangelize, he has to keep a mule, which is another big expense. Consequently, he hasn't money to make trips. We discussed various plans on how he might be able to visit more of his area of responsibility, but there were so many difficulties to face. He would have no money until the first of the month, and I had not come prepared to support more than Frisco and myself. Another worker, Heliodoro had not yet arrived from Chimaltenango; neither could I afford to wait. We prayed about it and then went to a meeting of the believers. There were over twenty present and quite a number of listeners stood in the street. We went to bed undecided, but trusting that the Lord would show us a plan.

Saturday, January 26. This morning we woke up with a plan well made out for us. I would write to Mr. Bishop for funds to support Heliodoro and a *mozo* and also for him to advance enough to *Don* Cipriano to make it possible for him to make his trip. He was to wait until Heliodoro and the money arrived and then start out with Heliodoro and a *mozo* on a trip through the northeastern end of his area.

Frisco and I were to leave immediately on a trip to the coast through a number of large *fincas,* towns, and small cities. From the coast we were to work our way back up through coastal Jutiapa to Altescatempa, also arriving about the 17th. The believers wanted us to wait until Monday before leaving, but I didn't like the idea of losing a day, so I turned a blind eye to their tears and we were off by 12:30.

We followed the road back toward Guatemala for about three miles, then turned off among some large coffee *fincas*. At the first *finca* we were well received. It was suppertime when we arrived at the second, so we ate a little before visiting houses. Most everyone was quite fanatical and few could read. One fellow asked me to read to him and then drew his machete, trying to scare me. I kept on reading without emotion. When he saw that his bluff didn't work, he asked for the paper, grabbed it, tore it up, cursed and stamped his foot, I asked the blessings of God upon him, then passed on. It was beautiful moonlight, so we hit the trail again until we came within earshot of the next *finca*. We made camp in a beautiful coffee grove, and here we visited all day Sunday.

— 12 —

OPEN TO NEW IDEAS

Their daily routine seldom changed. They ate mostly the plain food of the rural Indian peasant farmer, and as they moved from plantation to plantation, town to town and village to village, Cam and Frisco openly confessed, to all who would listen, their personal faith in Jesus Christ.

Their words weren't vague or unformulated. They were simple and straightforward: Jesus Christ is God's Son. The Bible presents God's message to mankind and by personal faith and belief in Jesus Christ, all people can have eternal life.

Cam also continued to record the natural phenomena of the land. His upbringing on the farm in Southern California gave him a natural curiosity about the configuration of the land.

He noted the trails and roads and how they flowed in and out of gullies and around the hillsides. He noticed symmetry and design. He spoke about coffee groves and rejoiced when he saw them flourishing rich, green and well-managed. Where the land was barren or abused he expressed sadness with the same concern as when he witnessed Indians being ill-treated, abused and neglected.

Cam wrote about skies filled with clouds and

moonlit nights bright as day with a pale white
light. He was surprisingly well-informed and aware
of all that was happening around him.

Yet like the lifestyle he lived and the words he
spoke, Cam was a plain man. It could be said of
him as it was once said of St. Francis of Assisi,
"Thou are not a man either comely of person, or
of noble birth, or of great knowledge; whence
then comes it that all the world runs after thee?"

All the world didn't run after Cam Townsend, of
course, but he did have, and continues to have, a
profound influence on thousands of lives. Several
incidents that happened shortly after he and Frisco
left on their journey toward El Salvador give us a
clue as to why Cam's influence grew to be larger
than himself.

January 28, 1918. We were on the road by 6:45
a.m. At the first house we found some *tamales* left over
from Sunday. (*Tamales* are seldom encountered here
except on Sundays and fiesta days.) After a short distance, we arrived at a small town scattered along a road
between the barren hills. Here we sold four Testaments
and stirred up considerable interest. As I was speaking,
a man came up to me and asked if I would read from the
Bible. I did. But after listening to me for a short time,
he quietly drew his long machete out of its scabbard
and raised it as if to strike me. I gulped a little, said a
prayer and continued to read. After a few moments,
the man lowered his machete and walked away. I do believe God protects us in all circumstances of our lives.

Sometime later, an Indian friend told me how he had
been returning from market and met a friend from his
pre-conversion days. This friend hailed him from the
door of a saloon and asked him to drink with him. The
Indian believer refused. This angered the other man

and he struck the believer with his machete. The believer dodged the blow and grabbed the other man around the waist and threw him to the ground. While he held his old friend on the ground, he preached the gospel to him. So forceful was the believer's witness that the man became convicted, cried out and asked for forgiveness.

A mile or so down the road, we came upon a *finca* just as the workers were being paid. They all gathered around and listened -- about sixty in all. As I spoke, one of the workers said to Frisco, "The words the American speaks sound like truth to me. How can a foreigner say such beautiful things?" Said Frisco, "The words you are hearing are not really the words of a man. It's God's Holy Spirit that speaks through the man about our Lord Jesus Christ." "Well, then," said the man, "we must be respectful and listen."

As we left the *finca*, a worker suggested we visit the town of Pueblo Nuevo. "It's just a short distance down the road," he said. Frisco and I agreed to visit the town even though it was a little out of the way of our prescribed route.

We walked some distance and at the base of a high mountain came to a fork in the road. From a passerby, we learned the town of Pueblo Nuevo was another four miles away, straight up the side of the mountain. Since we had promised the worker we would visit the town, we felt we should honor our word. However, as we struggled up the long hard trail, I began to wonder why the Lord was dragging us out of our way up this steep mountainside for just one town.

After we arrived, we spoke to a woman in a store and sold her two Testaments. As we talked, another woman overheard our conversation and invited us to her store next door. To our surprise, we learned she was a believer who had fled the earthquakes in Guatemala City.

She was overjoyed to see some "brothers" so far from the big city and invited us for lunch. We had eaten our lunch halfway up the mountain so we declined, saying we would like to visit the remainder of the town.

Near the outskirts of the town we came to a trail leading further up the mountain. Frisco didn't think there were houses up there, and we were about to pass by when I looked and saw a brood of chickens scratching on the trail. I concluded this meant a house, and we went up.

The family invited us inside and were deeply interested in all we had to say. The man said for a long time he had been hoping to hear about such things. We explained the gospel very carefully and finally he accepted Christ with joy. By 5:30 we had practically completed the town, selling three more Testaments, making nine for the day. We returned to the little store and found supper ready for us. When the woman couldn't persuade us to stay for two or three days, she fixed us a fine lunch for the next day.

Since the town was so high, and I had only one blanket, I decided we had better get down to a warmer climate before stopping for the night. Accordingly, after supper we closed the store long enough to have a little service. I read the eighth chapter of Romans, then we sang some hymns and prayed around. As we left, the woman gave me a twenty-five peso bill. I promised to telegraph her from Chiquimula when we arrived. It did us all good to find a fellow believer. Frisco was especially delighted, so much so, he wanted to stay for awhile.

It was shortly after seven o'clock, and the moon was just coming up when we hit the road again. The local druggist told us the next *finca* was three or four miles down the road and that the proprietors were Germans. When he learned I was an *evangélico* he said I would be safe in going as they were also *evangélicos*.

The moon shone brightly, and we made good time, arriving shortly after eight. The administrator came to the door and wanted to know in German if I "sprechen sie deutsch." When I told him I was an American, he showed a little warmth and took us up the hill to the home of the owner. We were received with equal warmth. My thoughts of Christian brotherhood fell considerably when they offered me a drink. When a *refresco* [soft drink] was offered, I accepted and when milk was named, I was delighted. The owner then called his daughter, and she served us some fine milk and cookies. Afterward they showed us to the guest room where the two of us slept like babies.

Tuesday, January 29. In the morning, as I was too late with my shaving to eat with the men, I accompanied the ladies. They spoke English quite well. Both were from Mexico, and one of them acted as tutor to the children of the family. They think Mexico is a paradise. After breakfast, the mother who made up some for the *evangelisticism* that the father lacked, fixed up a two-meal lunch. We then began work among the homes of the laborers.

One woman listened to the plan of salvation and was deeply convicted of her sins. We prayed with her and some of her friends, and she prayed, "Lord, forgive me." After professing Christ, she understood that it would be best to quit smoking and drinking and said she would try to get her "husband" to agree to a marriage. The custom for the poor is to live together without a legal marriage. Of the forty laborers on this *finca*, only two were legally married. The rest call themselves bachelors, and yet they call the women they live with their wives. For all practical purposes, these people are married. However, many hold in reservation the fact that they are not legally married to use in case of a quarrel!

I was astounded to learn that Frisco hasn't arranged his marriage yet. He says it is a custom in his town among the unconverted to spend two hundred days wages on liquor and food besides the legal fee. Then, too, the government takes a good bit of their time arranging the papers. If one wants the priest to marry them, the expense is about double. As a result, only the rich marry in the traditional method.

The notion that a man and a woman might, with the consent of their immediate community, commit themselves in marriage without the formal sanctions of a traditional church wedding, was at first difficult for Cam to understand. Then as he thought through the implications and observed their lifestyle, he was able to conclude that "indeed they do get along pretty well."

Principle of openness to new ideas.

While Mr. Townsend always advocated obedience to the law of the land in whatever country he served, this incident reflects openness and willingness to accept new ideas.

During the mid-1960's, a number of younger Wycliffe and SIL members had come into leadership within the two organizations. Geographical distance and the rapid growth of the organizations had precluded many of the new leaders from knowing Mr. Townsend in an intimate way. Often these new leaders were unaware of how the principles of the two organizations had been developed and forged into a working reality.

On one particularly difficult issue debated on the conference floor, Dr. John Beekman* (chief

---

*See the John Beekman story, *The Man With the Noisy Heart*, Moody Press, 1979.

translation consultant), a wise and insightful man, brought into perspective some of the important principles upon which Mr. Townsend had founded the two organizations. "What most of us fail to recognize," said John, "is that Uncle Cam is always about twenty years ahead of us in his thinking and planning."

One reason why that statement is true is that Mr. Townsend never lost the freshness of his youth, even into his eighties. His inquiring mind was always attracted to new ideas that would promote and extend the kingdom of God through Bible translation.

Cam and Frisco continued to work their way toward the coast in the direction of El Salvador. On their way, they passed around the foot of the great Tecamburro Volcano and through the edge of the coastal forests toward the town of Chiquimula, a distance of one hundred twenty-five miles from Guatemala City. It was then, as now, a handsome, well-laid-out colonial city with thick-walled adobe homes and *haciendas.*

Foremost in Cam's memory of that area were four notable experiences. The first took place three miles outside Chiquimula the night before they actually arrived.

Thursday, January 31. We were told there was a small ranch a few miles outside Chiquimula and it was here we planned to spend the night. The moon hadn't risen when we started on our way, and we had to use our flashlights to pick our way over the difficult rocky trail. When we arrived at the ranch, a woman came to the door with a light and a club. After I explained what we wanted, she lowered her club and a man, stark naked except for a waist cloth, stepped out of the darkness with a machete in his hand. He showed us some trees where I strung my hammock and Frisco made his bed. The mosquitoes and other insects were terribly thick. I spread my newly-acquired mosquito netting over the hammock, but they seemed to bite right through. At first I told Frisco the mosquitoes sang pretty well but bit like the devil. However, along toward morning, I decided that their song sounded more like the chant of a thousand whispering demons. I think, too, that ants got into the hammock for I was being bitten all night long. I was foolish enough to scratch which only made blisters all over my body. A few days later I set my mind on not scratching and now I'm not bothered much. To add to our misery, a primitive oxen-powered sugar mill worked all night somewhere in the vicinity. It made an awful squeaking noise. I don't know why they happened to be so energetic as to work at night.

The second experience that stood out for Cam was his first taste of iguana meat.

This is a lizard-like animal about three feet long and tastes halfway between chicken and fish. It was fine and I ate aplenty.

The third experience was more of an observation, but it was important because it reinforced the growing conviction in Cam's mind that Indian people needed to be reached with the good news of the gospel in their own mother-tongue language.

There are a great many Indians in this area who speak their own language. It was impossible for Frisco or myself to understand a word of their language.

The fourth and most memorable experience occurred a day and a half away in the then-dilapidated town of Cerritos. Cam described their walk from Chiquimula to Cerritos as one that "afforded them no shade from the blazing sun." Cam had been given the name of a man who was interested in the gospel and he and Frisco immediately called on him. He was most hospitable – but very drunk.

Don Cipriano had given me the name of a believer who received us with warm hospitality, although he was trying to sleep off his drunkenness in preparation for the evening festivities. Frisco and I left him sleeping and worked the town.

There are only a few huts in Cerritos. Most of the people don't seem to have anything to do except to drink booze. In one saloon the keeper was so pleased with our visit that he wanted to treat Frisco and me to a drink of rum!

We returned to our friend's house in the late afternoon, very tired and hungry. But the moment we returned, the man, now quite composed, invited a group of his friends in to hear the gospel. One of the men who came to the Bible study was quite drunk and insisted I speak to him. I was completely exhausted and could do nothing more than read the third chapter of First John. This touched him deeply, and he burst into tears and begged me to go with him to his home and explain this message to his mother. He said he only lived about three or four miles away.

What could I do but go with him? He had a pony but was so drunk he could hardly stay in the saddle. After about a mile, the man invited me to ride double with him and I happily accepted. Near to where he lived, we came to two large rivers. I was glad for the aid of the pony to ford them.

When finally we reached his home, the man's mother was overjoyed that I had shown an interest in her son.

She explained he had been a slave to drink ever since childhood. She lamented the fact that her son's wife and children often went without clothes and food because her son spent everything he earned on drink.

Before I left, the family called together a number of their friends and neighbors, and I conducted a little Bible study and prayer service. When I left, the mother, deeply touched by my visit, gave me a proper *abrazo* [hug], six eggs, and the equivalent of fifteen cents. The son, who by now was quite composed, asked me to pray for him that he would remain true to the confession of faith he had made during our time of study and prayer.

Cam kept his promise and prayed for this man. A year later almost to the day, Cam returned to Cerritos and inquired after the man who had been the notorious drunkard. "Yes," said the people, "we know who you mean, but he no longer becomes drunk as before."

Curious to see for himself, Cam revisited the man's house and discovered from his family that while he might, under pressure from his friends, take a glass or two, he no longer came home drunk. Cam saw evidence of his changed life in his wife and children. They were all well-clothed.

When Cam asked about the New Testament he had given to him, the man said that since he didn't know how to read, his fanatical sister had torn it up. He then asked Cam if he would once again tell him the story of salvation. With joy Cam again explained the compelling story of god's gift of love and grace to man through Christ's sub-stitutionary death on the cross, and the special place of fellowship and availability of God's strength to live a life that honors God through the power of the Holy Spirit. And then Cam left.

I had walked about two miles when I was surprised
to see the very man I had left running after me with
the New Testament I had given him in his hand. When
he came to me, he explained that his sister had threatened to destroy it again. Since he had promised me he
would take care of it, he wanted to return it before it
suffered harm.

During that year, God, in a remarkable way,
had answered Cam's prayer. As he bade farewell
all over again, he prayed that this man, who was so
removed from the inspiration and nurture of the
written Word, would be encouraged and sustained
in his faith.

From Cerritos, Cam and Frisco headed back
toward the mountains. They had decided not to
enter El Salvador by way of the coast. Since they
were to meet *Don* Cipriano in the town of Altescatempa before going into El Salvador, they chose
to go via a trail that led them across two large
rivers and through a forest of hardwoods to the
town of Pasaco, a distance of fifteen miles from
Cerritos.

Cam's diary reveals that when they arrived in
Pasaco, the man to whom they had been directed
wasn't at home, but his wife furnished them with
plenty of beans and tortillas and thus he went
to bed contented.

His diary also reveals that after a while it became apparent that the place was infested with
fleas and mosquitoes.

These pests were so bad that Frisco passed a very
poor night. My hammock and netting kept me pro-
tected from the pests until about three in the morning

when somehow they got inside. From then on it was one continual fight until daylight with a foe that I could hear and feel, but could not see.

— *13* —

THE EL SALVADOR AND HONDURAS CROSSING

"**O**bserve the experience, discover the principle and then invest that principle in your life." I don't know if Mr. Townsend ever explained his *modus operandi* in quite so clinical a fashion. His reasons for why he did what he did were most often an extension of his basic character, an intuitive response that only later, when observed by others, were enunciated into working principles.

Perhaps one exception to this was the principle, "Never lose your patience and be scrupulously courteous."

Longtime observers and friends would agree that Mr. Townsend did indeed live by this principle of courtesy. He continually urged the Wycliffe family to be particularly courteous to people in their host countries.

On one occasion I drove Mr. Townsend to a public phone in Mexico City where he was to make an important and urgent call. When we arrived, the phone was occupied by a woman who talked at great length about a variety of trivia. Mr. Townsend stood quietly to one side and without agitation, waited patiently until she was finished.

I was not as composed. The longer the woman

chattered, the more agitated I became. "Didn't she know who it was that stood waiting to make an important call while she chattered?" I thought. Finally the woman hung up the receiver. Mr. Townsend smiled, tipped his hat, bowed slightly and politely asked if she needed to make any further calls. In that one incident, he taught me a whole theology of courtesy!

Cam's courtesy, however, wasn't always this sensitive and spontaneous. It took practice, growth and maturity and a willingness to discard character traits that were mistakes against the life of faith and trust in Jesus Christ. The following incidents reveal how he shaped this ethic of courtesy into the fabric of his personal life and practice.

In the town of Chiquimula Cam encountered a parade honoring the local saint and was immediately confronted with two problems. If out of courtesy he doffed his hat as every man was doing as the image passed in front of them, he would, in his mind, compromise his faith. If he did not doff his hat, he most surely and obviously would be guilty of a serious breach of local courtesy. Cam solved both problems by deftly ducking inside a store so that, "I wouldn't have to take my hat off to the image."

However, several days later, Cam wasn't as willing to bend to local protocol, particularly if it required him to interrupt his lunch. On Wednesday, February 7, he and Frisco worked their way toward the Salvadorian frontier. As they came closer and closer to the border, the towns became smaller and more isolated, and the rejection of their message more vigorous. Not only was their message rejected, no one would sell them anything to eat, not even a tortilla. Finally in one town before they entered El Salvador, Cam presented himself and his passport to the local police chief, or *comandante*. He had learned his lessons well from the encounter in the highlands during his first attempt as a colporteur when he failed to ask permission of the local officials.

The *comandante* examined Cam's passport and gave him and Frisco permission to pass out tracts and sell their Scripture portion booklets. Before embarking on their assigned task, they decided they needed something to eat, no matter how meager. But in hut after hut, the two men were refused food and a hearing of their message. Finally, people in the second to the last hut in the town granted them a scant meal.

Exhausted and ravenously hungry, Cam was just about to dip his first tortilla into his bowl of steaming black beans when a soldier came and asked the two men to appear immediately in the office of the mayor to present his passport and explain why they were in town. Considering it a trivial request (after all, he had already presented his passport and explained his mission to the *comandante*), Cam said, "Later when I have finished my meal, I'll come." When at last he had satisfied his hunger, he presented himself at the office of the mayor who was "busy" with a number of lesser officials. In a kind of tit-for-tat game, the mayor properly impressed Cam by keeping him waiting for some time!

February 7, 1918. I confess this added waiting forced me to ask the Lord for more grace. When I was finally told the mayor would receive me, I stood before the assembled group of officials to explain why I was in their town.

I felt a little like Paul before King Agrippa* because the Lord gave me the words to speak. With great patience I explained the way of salvation and why I felt it was important for all people to be personally reconciled to God through His Son, Jesus Christ. I then spoke about the necessity of everyone having his own portion of God's Word. I explained the wonders of the Bible and drove home my point by reminding them that President Wilson and King George were constant readers of the Bible and that it would be most appropriate for his honor the mayor, together with his under officers, to do likewise.

The results from this presentation were better than expected. The mayor bought my last two New Testaments. God had turned defeat into victory!

Cam had accomlished a major coup in selling his New Testaments to the mayor, yet he and Frisco felt a deep hostility in the town and decided to leave by twilight. They walked for some time and came to what appeared to be nothing more than two cow trails. There were no markers and no one from whom to ask directions. The only recourse was to kneel and pray.

After we had prayed, it seemed clear to both of us that we should take the trail to the right, and we did.

The trail was narrow and rutted and hard to walk on in the dark and we picked our way along with the aid of our flashlights. As we walked, I suddenly spotted two white objects on a big rock at the side of the trail. We stood still and I held up my light. Finally one man stood up and then another. We greeted them and then passed on. Frisco said later they were probably there with an evil intent, but light had frightened them.

---

*Acts 25:23-27; 26:ff.

After spending the night behind a chicken roost on the outskirts of the small village of Palo Blanco, Cam and Frisco forded the River Paz and entered the Republic of El Salvador. Their destination was six miles away in the little town of Ahuachapan and then on to the railway city of Sonsonate. As they walked (and walking was becoming more and more painful for Cam; he had acquired ten large, painful blisters on his feet), they debated what it was they had been fed for breakfast that morning.

February 8. I'm afraid we left Palo Blanco with uncomplimentary thoughts. The people wouldn't listen to the gospel and at the place we slept, I asked for beans and the woman gave us some strange kind of meat. I claimed it was dog ribs because they were very skinny, just the size of an ordinary dog, and I knew the people would get a great delight in seeing us eat *chu chu* [dog]. Frisco thought it was either a very skinny pork or some mountain game. At any rate, it was only half enough to fill us and we went on our way looking for bananas or something else to fill us up.

At one place along the trail, we came to a squeaking sugar mill run by oxen. The men offered us a drink of sugar cane juice after I took a picture of the mill. I thought it was fresh, but when I tasted it, it bit, and I told them so and returned the cup. They all laughed and told me the juice had been kept to one side to ferment.

Another incident that took place on the El Salvador crossing was Cam's torn pants. He caught them on what he said was probably the only piece of barbed wire on the trail.

When we came to a lonely place on the trail, I got out a needle and thread from my sewing bag and mended the tear. The trousers I am wearing on this trip were given to Rob by the blacksmith back on the ranch in Corcoran [in California]. Rob laundered them and gave them to me when my khakis shrunk up too small.

On the morning of February 9, Cam and Frisco passed Lake Ahuachapan and entered the city of the same name through its large and imposing city gate. True to his interest in the topography of the land, in architecture and all that was going on about him, Cam noted the manicured parks and plazas. He recorded that shops and stores showed prosperity and that prices were high. He noted also that foreigners were not as highly respected in El Salvador as they were in Guatemala. "A soldier hissed at me off the sidewalk when I attempted to pass the government palace."

Painfully impeded by the blisters on his feet, Cam and Frisco left Ahuachapan for Sonsonate.

Saturday, February 10. The road to Sonsonate passed over a low range of mountains. This afforded us a beautiful view of the coffee *fincas* and the city below with the lake and mountains of Guatemala in the background.

The road up the mountain was good, but the descent was filled with ruts and terribly dusty. I was carrying a thirty-pound pack and although we were extremely tired and I could hardly walk because of my blisters, we pushed on in hope of making the twenty-eight miles that day. However, at six o'clock, we were still four or five miles outside the city and we decided to find a place to sleep. We did, made our beds and went to sleep.

After Cam hobbled into Sonsonate, he paid an overnight visit to his colleague Mr. Wilson of the Central American Mission. Said Mr. Wilson, "You have grown so much fatter, I would hardly have recognized you!"

For reasons unknown, on Sunday, February 11, Cam and Frisco split up for a short time. Frisco left Sonsonate by rail for the town of Santa Ana, and Cam took a train to the capital, San Salvador. His only major comment about that trip was that after distributing tracts through the cars, he sat down to watch the scenery. Part of that scenery included crossing over an immense lava bed created by a nearby volcano that a year earlier had spouted lava, covering trees, farms and ravines with a sea of molten rock for a distance of two to three miles.

After arriving in San Salvador, Cam made a brief tour of the city noting that it was about two-thirds the size of Guatemala City, and that it had recovered more quickly from the devastation of the December and January earthquakes.

The next entry in Cam's journal was exactly a month later on March 11. He was, however, faithful in corresponding to the "home folks."

His February 26 letter, written on leftover *Pacific Mail* stationery (the ship he had taken out of San Francisco), told of his return to Guatemala City the previous evening and about his plans to spend the next few days planning his proposed trip to Honduras with Mr. Butler.

Part of the letter also had to do with his excitement over the standard price of land – $5.00 per acre – and how profitable cattle raising would be. Then like a shrewd enterpreneur, he asked his parents if they knew anyone who would like to invest a few hundred dollars.

I know a place where I can buy some cheap land at about $2.00 per acre. I would only spend my vacations on it, but when it gets fixed up, I would want you to come down. A person could easily double his capital every two years. We can get two crops of corn a year, and I found a cotton-like substance growing on small trees. It would be splendid for comforters and pillows. I would like Paul to take it to Professor Smiley and get his opinion. Let me know soon.

> Then in classic statement that reflected Cam's growing interest in commerce, he said, "Can you send me a #791 flashlight? I sold mine for $2.75. It cost $1.00."

> His March 6 letter tells of a number of Christmas packages he had received (they had been delayed because of the earthquakes). He commented about feasting on raisins and walnuts. He was particularly pleased with a new pair of leggings given to him by Rob, a new watch and his new khaki suit.

I cut a handsome figure. If I had more time, I am pretty sure I could break a heart or two. Happy, too, for the razor blades. They will come in mighty handy. I am not famous for the frequency with which I shave. However, I haven't had the nerve to let my whiskers grow out as yet.

> One paragraph was particularly poignant and revealed something of his need to be loved and close to the ones he cared for. It also showed his growing uncertainty about the future.

I hate to say it again, but I haven't heard from you since last January 10. Rob can count on getting a letter every week from a certain girl in the States. He says she prays for him always. I wish you folks would follow suit. I will do some hard praying at this end of the line. I also wish you folks were down here. I would be perfectly happy to stay right through without returning to the States. At present I am up in the air about the future. If I don't finish college next year, I don't know when I will finish.

Then in an abrupt turnaround, without any explanation, Cam comes to the conclusion that it was out of place to try to mix God and money in mission work.

With regard to investments down here, I have decided that it is better to stay out of commercial affairs altogether when serving the Lord, except for very special reasons.

I truly do need your prayers. I am learning a lot of important lessons and mission practices. I also feel the weight of responsibility for a number of the Indian workers. Mr. Butler and I will leave for Honduras Monday or Tuesday. Frisco and a new worker called José will also go out by different roads. I am finding it hard to keep up my diary.

His trip to Honduras was first by rail from Guatemala City through Chiquimula to Santa Rosa and then to Morales, a distance of 170 miles from the capital. True to his character, Cam commented about every detail of the long trip. He marveled at the engineering feat of the railway builders as the train made its way through long tunnels as it looped its way down the side of a five-thousand-foot mountain to sea level.

In order to reach a particular gold mine, their last destination before entering Honduras, Cam and Mr. Butler rode four and a half miles on the United Fruit Company's narrow gauge banana train. Cam's only comment about discrepancy of wealth was that it was obvious who had the most money since the fruit company's bridges were all made from steel.

The train stopped at a *hacienda* three miles from the mine. Their host at the *hacienda,* the owner of the mine, was a Mr. Quimby who, along with Mrs. Quimby, "entertained us courteously. We each had a bed with springs and two clean sheets to remind us of home."

Mr. Quimby had tried to dissuade the men from taking the mountain trail into Honduras. "It's almost impassable, so much so, I wouldn't even want my mules to try it." That had been Mr. Quimby's assessment over dinner the evening before. Now on the morning they had planned to leave, Cam and Mr. Butler received an unexpected telegram informing them that the Indian man who had been sent to meet them at the border with mules had been unable to get through and was waiting for new instructions across the border in Honduras at Los Tarros. There was no alternative but to look to Mr. Quimby for help.

Thursday, March 13. Mr. Quimby was a fellow American and a native of California. When we told him of our circumstances, he said that while he didn't think we should go, he would nevertheless loan us three mules and a guide for the first day's journey.

After sending a telegram to the *comandante* in Los Tarros asking him to send our Indian man back to the border, we left the *hacienda.* And then I knew why Mr. Quimby had warned us not to go by this trail. We had no sooner started to ascend the hill when we entered a dense tropical forest. We were not to emerge for the next day and a half.

At times the undergrowth was so thick it closed in behind Mr. Butler and blocked my vision of him, even though he wasn't more than twenty-five feet in front of me. The trail was terribly muddy, and in some places the mules sank in past their knees. In other places, the mules had to step among the roots of trees to get around the holes. Often they were forced to step over fallen logs into mud holes.

On steeper climbs and descents, we dismounted and walked. It was too dangerous and almost impossible to ride. Once when I was walking, the mule slipped and fell. On another occasion, the cinch strap broke and the saddle slid off and I along with it. The mules seemed more like goats as they clambered up the steep climb. Drinking water was almost non-existent, and since grass wouldn't grow in the deep shade, the poor animals went hungry.

We met no one until evening when the Indian man met us with fresh mules. That night we made camp on a small river that forms the boundary of Guatemala and Honduras. As we sat around the campfire, the guides told us stories of the many jaguars that inhabit the surrounding forests. Accordingly, Mr. Butler and I followed their suggestion to place our hats on sticks so the animals would leap at the hats instead of on us.

The weary pair entered Los Tarros about midday and were delighted to eat their first meal since about 5:00 the day before and sell five New Testaments.

Since Mr. Butler was the senior man on this trip, it was he who preached in the town plaza and it was Cam who gave out tracts to the passersby and those who stood to listen.

Afterward, they hurried on to work the small and scattered villages on their way to a place called Colinas where Mr. Butler was to be a missions conference speaker.

The trails to Colinas were very difficult. Most seemed to go straight up. The hours in the saddle were hot and long, generating hearty appetites in both of us. The difficulty was that food was hard to find. At one place, all I could find was eggs. I ate six. At another place, all we had was one tortilla and roasted river crabs. Thus it was a tired, dirty and hungry pair that rode into Colinas on our second day into Honduras.

Cam's journal and letters give few details about what he and Mr. Butler spoke about on that trip. It is clear, however, that Cam's love, respect and admiration for the mission leader was growing, and he wanted to learn all he could from him. It was also clear that this trip, plus the trip to El Salvador and all Cam had done during his few short months in Guatemala, reaffirmed Mr. Bishop's growing conviction that Cam would make an ideal career missionary. In a letter, Cam related this along with his deepening interest and concern for Guatemala's Indian people and his dream for himself and for his family.

Morales, Guatemala
March 13, 1918

. . . In a conversation with Mr. Butler, he said he would like me to consider joining the Central American Mission if I thought it was the Lord's will. Let me tell you the plan I've been keeping before the Lord; I want to know what you think of it. First, there is a wonderful opportunity here for someone to work among the Indian people. Why couldn't you, Mama, Papa and Paul, come down next year? I know of one of the prettiest spots in Guatemala. It's around Antigua and San Antonio. It's healthy, living is cheap, there are good medical facilities in Antigua, and I could build you a house (earthquake proof) and we will all just camp down here until the war is over, or the Lord comes back.

Paul could work with the Bible House for the first six

months, learn the language, and then we all could work together in the mission work, Paul taking the preaching and I more the itinerant work. If the Lord will, we could start a little school that would serve the Indians. I have to tell you the Indian work has been on my heart for a long time now. I believe we together could do a great work.

The letter continued with great enthusiasm describing the good roads around Antigua and how he could secure a horse and buggy, and what an ideal vacation spot it would make for everyone.

No one was missed. Papa could plant a garden and work as much ground as he wanted. There would be a servant girl who spoke English for Mama, and Paul would never forget or regret such an experience. Even Cam wasn't left out. He concluded by promising that he and Paul could complete their college work after the war. He then left Psalm 55:22 as his closing benediction: "Cast all your burden upon the Lord and he shall sustain you."

Little did Cam realize that in less than a year he would realize his dream of owning and living in a house in San Antonio, but it wouldn't be with his mother and father and brother.

— 14 —

I'LL BE TWENTY-TWO
ON TUESDAY

Although it didn't reach riot proportions, there was confusion, pushing, shouting and fist-clenched threats against him. But early in this part of his career, it had become a matter of conscience. He simply could not remove his hat for an idol.

> Colinas, Honduras
> March 20, 1918

... The fiesta was taking place at the same time as our conference in Colinas. At each corner of the plaza stood a booth with a doll representing a special saint. At each of the booths and in front of the church, a soldier was stationed to ensure that passersby would show proper respect. I'm afraid I caused something of an uproar when I passed by and didn't doff my hat.

Cam's first trip to Honduras lasted a little more than a month. It was on this trip Cam received a seed thought that blossomed into a most important mission strategem, namely, the place of women in missionary ministry. In a letter home he revealed his new thinking.

... I was especially impressed with the zeal and courage of a particular woman missionary I met at the conference. She travels fearlessly all over the country. Her untiring labors have resulted in a string of congre-

gations. From what I have seen of the women missionaries, they are putting the men to shame.

Eighteen years later, in 1936 when Eunice Pike
and Florence Hansen (now Mrs. George Cowan)
presented themselves as the first women candi-
dates for mission work under the auspices of the
fledgling Summer Institute of Linguistics, co-
founder, L.L. Legters, vigorously opposed the idea
of women doing pioneer mission work. Not so Mr.
Townsend! He had seen women at work in Central
America and was convinced from experience that
God could and would lead and guide a woman just
as He would a man. Mr. Townsend prevailed, and
of course the rest is history. He demonstrated once
again that he was indeed twenty years ahead of
the thinking of his contemporaries.

There was yet another experience on that trip to
Honduras. It didn't have any significant spiritual
value, but it reflects both his pluck and determina-
tion to get on with whatever he was commissioned
by God to accomplish.

After leaving Colinas, we passed through Santa Bar-
bara and came to a large river. The only way for people
to travel in Honduras is by foot through the jungles or
by canoe. Here we were on one side of the river and the
canoes and ferry boat were on the other, but we
couldn't see anyone who would come and ferry us
across.

After calling for some time and getting no response,
and since it was growing late, I decided to find the
ferryman myself. Accordingly I stripped and swam the
stream. This so surprised the ferryman, who had been
watching us all the time from a secluded hut, that he
came on the run.

When I came to shore, he expressed great surprise at my foolhardy courage. "Don't you know the river is infested with alligators?" he said. I didn't tell him I didn't know, but as I reflected on what I had done, I thought of a certain young man in the Revolutionary War who had been given a young colt, both ugly and mean. One day the company commander gave the order to advance. Everyone obeyed until the enemy blocked their path at a bridge. At the first volley, the advancing company wheeled and ran. The colt, however, was too mean to turn. Desperately, the frightened youth dug in his spurs. Immediately the colt tore over the bridge toward the enemy at full speed. The youth's seemingly courageous act struck fear into the enemy, and his comrades turned and followed him.

It was an easy victory for which the frightened youth was made a colonel. He never revealed that he owed it all to the colt. Thus it was with me – my bravery was due only to ignorance.

Cam's last journal entry was March 13. He would not begin again with any regularity until May 10, 1918. We do, however, have his personal letters home for this "silent" period, and they reveal his growing conviction that he should continue on in Guatemala rather than return to finish his college education.

Chiquimula, Guatemala
April 15, 1918

Paul, when you become acquainted with the needs here and see this beautiful country, you won't be satisfied with work at home. But then, the Lord has a plan for each of us, and the successful life is the life spent according to that plan. . . . . I have used Papa as an illustration of a man who plants fruit trees for others to reap the harvest.

Guatemala City
April 24, 1918

. . . With regard to returning to college next year, I would never feel right about going to school when the world is in such great need of a Christian witness as it is today.

As concerning the army, I plan to work down here until I am actually called. When my turn comes, I can register here. In the meantime, I will be able to get in some good hard licks before my time comes. I know my country is in great need. You don't know how I would like to enlist, if that were permitted, or to enter the productive army, but I consider my duty for the present is to be here.

I do realize I need to finish my education, but I am sure another year of active experience will not hurt me. However, if you folk need me for financial support or for other reasons, I want you to let me know right away.

Guatemala declared war on Germany last Saturday. Most of Latin America will follow soon.

> At the bottom of the letter, Cam wrote a single sentence that revealed his growing interest in helping to educate children and young people who could not afford an education. "I have sent a girl from El Salvador to a mission school in Chiquimula, as well as a boy from Honduras." In later correspondence, Cam told how he met the boy.

On a ride to the ranch of a believer to secure a fresh mount, I met Rodolfo. He was a bright-eyed boy of twelve who told me he wanted to learn how to become a carpenter, but spent his days looking after two sheep. I became extremely interested in Rodolfo when I learned his mother (a loose-living woman) had turned him over to his uncle who had little interest in or compassion for the boy other than making him work as hard as possible.

When I approached the uncle about gaining his permission to take the boy to the mission school in Chiquimula, the uncle, to my surprise, said yes, and since I was paying for the boy's education, he promised to take his nephew personally to the school.

Out of my $25.00 per month salary, I am already supporting Frisco's daughter, but since living is cheap, I decided to tithe a second time. [A third child, a girl, was being supported by Cam's parents.]

Principle of taking God at His word.

From all the working principles enunciated by Mr. Townsend, five have been distilled into what has become known as Wycliffe's "Five Basic Principles." They are:

1. WE PIONEER. We go where the Word of God does not exist in the local language.
2. WE GIVE THE PEOPLE THE BIBLE, free from religious sectarianism. We do not propogate any brand of religion.
3. WE FOLLOW THE LINGUISTIC APPROACH. We enter a country as linguists and produce grammars and dictionaries in languages that have never been analyzed before.
4. WE SERVE EVERYBODY, friend or foe, as we are able. We prefer that our service be done under the umbrella of the host government.
5. WE TRUST GOD FOR THE IMPOSSIBLE. He can provide whatever is necessary to reach all the language groups of earth. He will open closed doors.

Perhaps Cam's May 7 letter pinpoints more than any other correspondence the experience out of which grew the principle of taking God at His word. It was a principle he never violated.

It was a great relief to learn you thought it was all right for me to stay another year. The way things are happening in the world, one has to take God at His word and decide on the spur of the moment.

My decision to go to Honduras came about that way. The Lord seemed to close all doors, but when I took the first step, He smoothed out the difficulties. After I arrived and saw how hard it was to get consent to come into the country, I knew the Lord had guided.

We know so little of the future. Things look as though the Lord could come at any moment and end all our troubles. In the meantime, let's be up and ready, willing always to take God at His word.

Many years later Mr. Townsend expressed this same theme to a group of new Wycliffe workers when he said: "Be willing always to take God at His word. Remember Jesus' words when He said, 'All power is given unto me in heaven and in earth, go therefore to every nation, to every tribe, to every language. I will open doors; I will provide the men and women; I will provide the officials to help; I will provide the money. Go! And lo I am with you always'" (Cam's paraphrase).

In the letter expressing their affirmation that he stay another year, Cam's parents also expressed their disappointment at not seeing him as soon as they had expected. However, his father's touching postscript reveals their special sensitivity to the way God was leading their son.

"May God direct you in everything you do. When you do God's will, you do mine, for I don't want you to do anything but His will. I want you to live for that end, and to the end that He has

created you – to bring honor and glory to God –
and I am glad you are doing so. (Mama says the
same as me.)

"I want you to be happy. Where you are, there is
much to make you sad and serious. I was most
afraid you couldn't be jolly and fun-loving anymore. I wouldn't want that. I'm glad to see you
haven't changed."

Jutiapa, Guatemala
May 17, 1918

Dear Home Folks:

It's nearly a year since I left home to work on the
ranch in Corcoran. I venture to say I have learned as
much in this year as in two or three years at college.
When a fellow once gets his purposes in life lined up
with God's purposes, there is little danger of his quit-
ting his studies to perfect himself in the Lord's work. I
learn fast now and retain longer than when I was in
school.

I am happy to say that when I didn't get in the way,
the Lord has used me to bless and encourage some
folks. Frisco told me the other day the first Indian man
I was able to win for the Lord came to a meeting with a
cut up face and black eye, all received because he is a
believer in Jesus Christ.

We took a new road to Jutiapa, one we hadn't worked
before. The first day we sold twelve New Testaments
(best yet). On Saturday we sold eight. Both ways we
walked over fifteen miles. The opportunities down here
are simply wonderful. I could never settle down to a
pastorate in the States unless, of course, the Lord made
it tremendously clear that He wanted me there, and I
don't anticipate that He will.

The people in Jutiapa are on fire for the gospel, and
very hospitable. The desire to start a school grows on

me every day. I think a school that would teach reading, writing and arithmetic together with agriculture and various trades such as carpentry, shoemaking and, of course, the Bible would be an unequaled force in evangelizing the Indians of Central America. Besides lifting them up socially, their own school would break down prejudice and open doors for Indian missions in other Indian towns. It is my belief that Indians make better missionaries than do Ladinos. The persecution doesn't phase them as much, at least this is true of the believers from Frisco's town. Please pray that a school may be established for the highland people.

During the middle of May, Cam's diary became more eloquent in what it didn't say, than what it said. The absence of long, detailed accounts of his daily activities revealed he was far too busy traveling and doing the work to take time to write. Often beside the date was a simple sentence telling the name of the town or *finca* he and Francisco had reached or were planning to reach. Sometimes there were only brief notes as in the case of May 19: "Two services, letters, boil getting worse."

In a later entry, Cam revealed this boil (on his arm) gave him great pain and that he also suffered from stomach problems. So severe were the stomach disorders that in the town of San José, about a day's ride northeast of Chiquimula, he had to stop. "Here the brethren put me to bed while the sisters prepared a tea of herbs."

Weak, yet eager to continue his colportage work, Cam again set out after a delay of three days. His stomach problems cleared, but he experienced continual discomfort from the boil.

For eleven days he tried to ignore the throbbing pain, until at last on May 30, he and Frisco entered the town of Candelaria for the second time, only because it was a good-sized town, and Cam would find a doctor to lance his boil. His only comment in his diary about the boil was that the doctor who lanced the boil was a "free thinker."

His other comment on his visit to Candelaria was that on the outskirts of town, he saw a *comandante* who recognized him from his earlier visit and the two had a pleasant and restful chat.

In a letter to his parents, Cam never once mentioned his stomach problems nor the pain he had suffered with the boil. These were eclipsed by two important purchases. The first was a "dandy jack-knife" to replace the one he had lost overboard on the trip down to Guatemala. The second was of considerably greater proportions.

Candelaria, Honduras
May 30, 1918

I had a great time buying a mule. I guess I surprised all my Indian friends by breaking all their records for quick buying. One morning I let it be known I was in the market for a mule. By 11:30 the mules began to come, and by one o'clock, I found one that suited me. By five o'clock, I paid my money and received the bill of sale. I would have been through earlier, but the transaction was delayed because in this town of sixty thousand and three banks, I couldn't find anyone who would cash a New York bank draft.

At last I had to sell it to a Turk (they, like the Chinese in Guatemala City, have a small trade monopoly) for four points below market price. The mule is fine and I have called her *Peregrina* (Spanish for pilgrim).

In short, terse sentences, however, Cam's diary told a slightly different story about the new and unexpected problems that went along with owning a mule.

June 4, 1918. Mule ran away. Caught her twice, but broke away each time. Returned two miles down a mountain trail, but sold five gospels in needy section doing it. Took bath in creek. Traveled one and a half miles under heavy rain. In a few minutes, trails were little rivers. Ate mangoes in dark. When someone brought a light as I was eating my seventh, I found it full of worms. Had thought them fine.

Cam's next letter home brought to light his life-long gift of encouragement and showed to what lengths he was willing to go to exercise and invest that God-given gift. After hearing that his missionary friends Mr. and Mrs. Aberle, hadn't seen another American in five months, Cam decided to take a three-day detour to visit and encourage them.

He was traveling with the boy Rodolfo and his uncle on their way back to the mission school in Chiquimula. With instructions that he would meet them in three days in the town of Copán, Cam made his way alone to the Aberles.

After his visit, Mr. Aberle, who had business to transact in Chiquimula, took advantage of Cam's company.

Dulce Nombre, Honduras
June 13, 1918

Mr. Aberle had only been over the trail once before and when we arrived at a certain town, we were unsure of the correct trail. We decided to ask the mayor and went over to what we thought was the town hall, a large, white building on the edge of the plaza. It wasn't. But since the road past the building looked well traveled, we decided it must be the correct one.

After a couple of miles, we came to a fork in the trail. We ignored the fork and followed what we thought was the main trail but after a quarter of a mile or so, it became evident we were on the wrong trail. We returned to the fork and followed the right-hand trail, but after following this trail for some distance, it soon became evident that we were still going the wrong way. Since it was such a great distance back to the town, we decided to keep on going believing God had led us in this direction for His purposes, and that He would get us back on the correct trail.

It was a wretched path, and after a long, rocky descent down a mountain, we came to a river and there found a hut. The men of the hut were in the fields working, and the woman said she couldn't give out the information I was asking for until the men came home. As Mr. Aberle and I discussed what we should do, a girl from another hut came and told us about a village a short distance away and a little-used trail that would take us back to the main trail.

We thanked her and found the village and trail just as she had told us. That night we stayed in a town where we discovered the people had never heard the gospel. After we attended to our mules, I began to play my harmonica. This attracted a large crowd. Afterward, Mr. Aberle and I were able to present a long and careful explanation of the gospel. To our extreme delight, one young man accepted Christ. And then we knew why we had gotten lost! It was that this man could find his way to eternal life.

In July, Cam wrote two letters – one letter to his parents that described a hair-raising river crossing with his new mule, *Peregrina;* the other to his brother Paul in which he congratulated him for joining the Student Volunteer Movement.

Cam then expressed hope that God would lead Paul to join him in Guatemala but quickly added, "But we must learn to wait His direction and follow it." Next came an extraordinary sentence that read, "I sometimes wonder if He may not want you in Russia. To my mind it is the most needy and neglected field in the world."

Cam concluded his letter to Paul with a rare glimpse of self-disclosure. It came after a short discourse on how deeply he felt about starting his school and how he might finance it.

Comayaguela, Honduras
July 7, 1918

. . . I could help the school with what I could save from my $25.00 a month allowance. Only the Lord knows what is best and I am learning to wait on Him. I just tell you folks all my dreams with the hope it will not make you all as visionary as I am.

The second letter dated July 7 to his parents began immediately with his description of trying to get across the Cospe River.

It had been raining heavily, and the mountain streams were swollen. The river we had to cross seemed formidable and I went in mounted on *Peregrina*, leading *Misionero*, our pack mule. All went well until I got to the center of the current. Here the water came up to my knees and into one of the saddlebags.

I knew *Misionero* would never make it with his load, and turned him loose. *Peregrina* nearly fell three times but recovered herself and we got out all right. *Misionero* stood on the edge of the current as if debating which way to go, and then made the decision to turn back.

I left *Peregrina* on the riverbank and returned via

the hammock bridge. (It's made of wire cables with board slats to walk on.) I unloaded *Misionero,* and Frisco and I carried the cargo across the bridge. Then I came back and tied a long rope to *Misionero.* Frisco was to lead him to the edge of the current and then throw the rope across to me.

It was a good plan, but it didn't work. The beast absolutely refused to enter the water again. Finally after all our urging, two women came to the stream to do their washing and when they saw our problem, helped drive *Misionero* into the water with sticks. Frisco was unable to get the rope to me, so I mounted *Peregrina* again, went into the river apiece, caught the rope, and after bracing myself against the rocks, pulled the struggling animal across with all my might.

We were just leaving when two other men with four mules attempted to cross and when one reached the swift current, he fell from his mule. He struggled for a bit but was able to swim ashore minus his hat. The other man went upstream to where the current was smooth and deep, took off his clothes and swam across.

Misionero went lame and had a large cyst on her back that I had to lance. Since the little animal was in no condition to travel far, Frisco and I split up. He worked Gracias and other nearby towns while I made my way to the capital.

It was a long, hard mountain journey of seven days over a rain-washed slippery, rocky wall. Often I would travel for hours alone through pine forests before I came upon a small village or town. Several times I lost my way.

Once when I was quite alone there came a flash and a crash. I thought I would fall off my mule! Not more than 200 yards away, a great pine tree had fallen. It sure knows how to thunder and lightning among these mountains.

The rain stopped during the last four days of my trip and this made traveling more delightful. The next to the last day I traveled forty-eight miles according to native calculations. I was on the trail and in the saddle for fourteen hours. *Peregrina* held up splendidly. I am certainly pleased with my buy.

Tegucigalpa is a beautiful little city snuggled in the mountains at the juncture of two streams. The section south of the river is called Comayaguela, where I am now, while the northern side is Tegucigalpa proper. A good stone bridge connects the two sections.

The Quakers have a good work in Tegucigalpa and I am staying here in Comayaguela with a family called the Lincolns. They are fine young missionaries. We had quite a celebration on the fourth that included ice cream, firecrackers and a benefit ball held for the Red Cross in the National Theater.

I expect Frisco to be here in a couple of days and then we will leave right away for Amapola* and that section of the country. I must close now. Studying for talks, writing letters and preparing for the trips leaves me little time. In some ways I feel like I am sixteen, but on Tuesday I'll be twenty-two. I wish I could celebrate with you.

Lovingly,
Cameron.

---

*This trip resulted in the sale of 101 New Testaments. "The Lord did more than I had asked or even thought," wrote Cam.

— 15 —

THE NEW VISION

Robbie, who had been working in Huehueten-ango, Guatemala, had returned for a short visit with Cam before he left to answer his army draft call. The two men celebrated with a feast of pork, rice and *tamales*. It would be two and a half years before the two men would see each other again. Cam kept looking for his own official draft letter, never knowing if he would be called in a month or six months. In the meantime, Cam went about preparing for a trip that would take him back to El Salvador and then into Managua, Nicaragua.

During his delay with the cargo mule back in July, Cam had stopped to give a tract to a man riding through on the trail. As the man turned to leave, Cam noticed a large fossilized tooth sticking out of his saddle bags and inquired about it. The man told him about a large hill of bones about a half-day's journey in the direction he was travelling. His curiosity piqued, Cam located a hill between Santa Rosa and Esperanza and found his own fossilized tooth that weighed about three pounds.

Several days later Cam met a mining engineer

who suggested that he write a description of the hill of bones and send it to the Smithsonian Institution. Acting on the engineer's suggestion, Cam sent in his report and in due course received a reply commending him and stating that the hill was an important discovery, and they were preparing to send an expedition to examine it further.

Cam's journeys in Honduras, El Salvador and Nicaragua from August to October 1918 were for the most part duplicates of all the other trips he had taken. The trails seemed to be more rugged in El Salvador and Nicaragua than in Guatemala. He wrote that in some places "the rocks were cutting poor *Peregrina's* hooves down to the quick."

In one town he was taken to military headquarters to explain his presence and show them his passport. After a careful scrutiny, he was released to continue on his journey. Before he left, Cam in his own inimitable way, began to share his faith with the *comandante*. Whereupon, the official abruptly touched his sword and grunted, "This is my creed."

In another town he was almost arrested because unknowingly he had stood in front of a soldier standing guard. He learned to his dismay that such a practice made him liable for arrest. However, he was merely pulled aside by another soldier and given a stiff warning never to do such a thing again.

Occasionally, Cam's long hot days were interrupted by a hunting expedition.

One afternoon I accompanied a local hunter upriver to hunt alligators. The alligators are plentiful but hard to kill, and my presence didn't change his luck. They always got into the water after he wounded them.

The iguana are very thick and I had fun throwing stones at them. I threw some rocks at an armadillo. Only his armor saved him! One night the hunter brought home a big iguana. It was quite a task to skin it.

While wild animals were plentiful and dangerous, it was most often the domesticated kind that gave Cam difficulty. During one overnight stay, after Cam unloaded his rawhide packsaddle and laid it on the open veranda (the usual and normal place for travelers to sleep and spend the night), a pack of village dogs picked up the scent of the rawhide, chewed off the thongs and badly damaged the entire saddle.

Often when the villagers learned that Cam and Frisco were *evangélicos* (some thought they were witches), no one would sell them food. On these occasions the two men frequently dined on raw eggs and what small pieces of bread or tortillas they could scrounge.

This problem of getting enough to eat was a continual and daily concern to Cam. Once he wrote, "I ate the last half of a tortilla and a small piece of sugar loaf, the last of our rations. We can get nothing to eat in this town, so that little bit had to suffice for over thirty-six hours."

Cam's faithful and dear friend Francisco Díaz was an indispensible partner to Cam's colporteur venture. Often Cam recorded that Frisco had sold more Scriptures and New Testaments than he had.

In every way Frisco is an equal colleague in my ministry, and in every way he is a prize. He is such a special friend to me. He always serves me willingly and cheerfully. He frequently gives me the needed inspiration to continue on. Our times of prayer and Bible study are especially precious. We often wish these times could be longer, but we always seem to be in a hurry to reach another town.

I often marvel at how God has used Frisco, an unsophisticated Indian man who lived all his life in a society that makes it a practice to taunt and oppress the Indian. It is a society that considers it a disgrace for a Spanish-speaking person to be seen talking with an Indian as man to man, they being considered only an animal. With all he has had to endure, God has taken Frisco and made him into a loving, caring man who takes responsibility for his own decisions, even when he has stumbled.

Once while he was working a town by himself and having good success giving out tracts house to house, the local priest heard about this and came to intimidate and frighten him away. He laughed and poked fun at Frisco, trying to make out he was just an ignorant Indian.

But like Peter and John of old, the bystanders and the priest were astonished at what came out of Frisco's mouth. He may be unlearned, but he is wise and possesses a remarkable understanding of theological issues. More importantly, he has received the Spirit of God and speaks in power and strength that goes beyond human wisdom. When the priest saw he was no match for Frisco's steadfastness, he changed his tactics. He patted Frisco on the back and admitted he was preaching truth, but if he would please stop enlightening his parishoners and leave town, he would give him three pounds of meat. It was a subtle temptation and Frisco, being only a year old in the faith, accepted. On reflection, he regretted giving in.

Daily there was the battle against the ever-present mosquitoes, ants and ticks (Cam was now taking quinine and it was causing nausea). And the mules were forever wandering away. Once when Frisco backtracked the mules for over an hour, he returned to tell Cam he had been unsuccessful and was going back out after them again and needed some rope. Cam immediately took this as the Lord's leading.

I had a feeling the Lord had wanted us to stay all night at the last settlement we had been at the day before to teach the people more instead of hurrying through. Thus I was glad for this opportunity to go back. Accordingly, we followed the trail back five miles. I stayed at the home of the man whom the Lord had put on my heart, and explained the way of salvation while Frisco kept looking for the mules. The man listened attentively, and I trust that by continued reading of the Scripture portions he bought and our prayers, he will believe.

Soon Frisco returned with the mules. Like us they had been bothered in the night with insects and had been rolling in the dirt to relieve the stings.

In ways similar to Sir Edmund Hillary and Norjay Tenzing, and Lewis and Clark, Cam and Frisco were dependent upon one another, not as master to servant, but as two free and equal men captivated by the knowledge that they were collaborators with God in an eternal quest. The object of their quest wasn't geography. Rather, it was to bestow the truth of God's love and care to a people suffering from poverty, disease and oppression. A people who lacked an understanding of the full message of new life and liberty that comes from a personal relationship with Jesus Christ.

In a candid and remarkably perceptive passage from his journal, Cam revealed how he had caught

a new vision for his life's ministry. While he
acknowledged God as the One who directed him
in all of life, he admitted the instrument God used
was Frisco, the man. It was Frisco whom God had
used to make him aware of a whole new level of
needs and values.

August 30, 1918. A subject Frisco and I frequently
discuss around the campfire and on the trails is the
need of Frisco's own people, the Cakchiquels. When
I observed the Indians in El Salvador and Honduras
and saw how they suffered less oppression and had
more freedom than the Indians in Guatemala, my heart
burned within me for Guatemala's suffering people.
And when I see how quickly Frisco learned and how
eager he was to follow the Lord and do His will, and
how many latent possibilities there are in him and his
people, I am stirred even further to recognize the need
among the Cakchiquel people.

I did a survey of all the missionaries who for years
have served faithfully in Guatemala, and almost none
of them have seen fit to learn any of the Indian languages. This means that sixty percent of the people in
this republic have no gospel witness. The reason for this
is the difficulty of learning the many different languages and dialects, all of which are unwritten.

I have come to realize that it is imperative this need
be surmounted in this generation and the people be
reached with the message of salvation. God has given
me youthful vigor, faith and a challenge. Therefore, I
have decided to devote my life to the evangelization of
the Indian peoples.

Frisco, of course, is gladdened to realize that his pale-
faced companion has come to this decision. This made
the rest of our trip so much lighter as we talked over
plans for the future of our work.

Since sales are becoming large enough to recover commissions (our commission is fifty percent of total sales over five dollars in any one month), we decided to save all our commission money and establish a fund toward establishing a school in San Antonio for the children of Indian believers.

After praying they both would be led to a home that would be prepared to receive the gospel, Cam and Frisco set out on their respective areas of service. From the town of Chinandega in El Salvador, Cam took an 8 a.m. Sunday train to Managua. In the meantime, Frisco remained behind to finish canvassing the town.

Cam's only remark about the train trip was that "it was a beautiful ride over nearly unbroken stretches of farmland." And that when they stopped for a twenty-minute lunch break, he treated himself to a good lunch. Good, except for the price. "I was charged sixty cents. I winced, and said to myself, never again. That is too large a slice out of my twenty-five dollars a month salary."

Several days later, Cam recorded that he had an appointment with a dentist who had been educated in the States and spoke English.

September 7, Managua, Nicaragua. It was a relief to get into the chair after having suffered at the hands of that roughneck American dentist in Tegucigalpa.

September 9. Several young people from the Baptist congregation – a young fellow, three girls and myself – all went rowing on Lake Managua. I bought a good-sized watermelon for ten cents, but in the end it cost me dearly. While using my new jackknife to cut open the watermelon, I dropped it overboard. When will I ever learn to keep a knife?

The remaining days in Managua were spent visiting several different mission works, including three Gospel Halls (Plymouth Brethren assemblies). He spent one fascinating afternoon watching how cattle were off-loaded from the sailing ships.

First a strong rope is tied around the steer's horns. Then he is hoisted up by a pulley until his whole weight is suspended by his horns and he clears the deck. The steer is then shoved out over the water and dropped in, making a big splash. Next a stevedore mounts the steer's back and guides the animal to shore. However, unless the rider is careful, some of the steers in blind fright swim in just the opposite direction.

Cam left Managua on September 16 in the company of a young Nicaraguan believer, Hipolito Osegueda, who wanted to accompany him as far as Honduras. Cam met Frisco in the town of Leon (he was looking after the mules there) and together all three started out on the 17th of September. After a long, hot nine-mile ride, the three were suddenly overtaken by a violent tropical rainstorm. Frisco had neglected to bring the rain capes and there was nothing but a tree to give them shelter. The result was a severe drenching.

Later when they arrived at the home of a believer, Cam was asked to conduct a meeting. He did, in his wet clothing. None of the men had a change of dry clothing. After the meeting, the weather turned chilly and almost as quickly as the changing weather, all three men came down with chills and fever.

For the next three days, Cam and Hipolito faded in and out of delirium. At one point Hipolito thought he most certainly was going to die. Frisco too was far from well. On the third night Cam traded beds with Frisco.

I decided my hammock was too cold and traded places with Frisco who had been sleeping on a plank that rested on a grain chest. It was the hardest bed I have ever slept on! Pine or hardwood springs are not so bad when you're well, but when you're sick, they are most uncomfortable.

I dreamed I went home and was in the parlor and my brother-in-law was throwing books in every direction. I started upstairs when he slammed a book that jarred me and I fell to the floor. I woke up and found myself on that same miserable old plank.

By the fourth day, Cam and the others were feeling some better and took a little food. In the middle of his convalescence, Cam wrote that on Sunday he was shocked by a neighborhood dance held in the believer's house.

I made the best of a bad thing by having the family give out tracts to the visitors. These are the first and only dancing Christians I have met in all of Central America. I suppose the reason for this is because they haven't been trained in the Word as carefully as they should. I was interested to hear how the father had given up his idol-engraving business after he accepted Christ.

On Wednesday, September 26, exactly a week later, the three men again started out on the trail. Cam and Hipolito took turns riding *Peregrina.* The trail was muddy and made it hard going for both man and beast. Exhausted, the travelers found lodging just before the late afternoon rain.

The people who offered the men shelter were so excited to have visitors, they talked the whole night through. "One woman," said Cam, "spoke like lightning at the top of her voice and said nothing. When she saw me nodding off to sleep, she promptly woke me up."

The following day the men crossed a great swampy plain Cam described as "fording a river of mud five miles wide." At one point in the ordeal, the mule slipped and fell on Hipolito. The mule wrenched her leg and Hipolito, though unhurt, refused to ride. In his weakness and exhaustion, Cam thought at one point he would never get across.

That night they stopped at a ranch house and were able to secure a few tortillas and cheese. Cam noted this was so much more palatable than the greasy pork and chicken the women had made for them to break their three-day fast after their sickness (he refused it).

After a twelve-mile hike through a drizzling rain, the men came to a place called Sauce. Here, in spite of the rain and the discovery that many in the settlement were sick with the same influenza that had struck Cam and the others, they sold "a great many books."

From Sauce they traveled a good many more miles until finally they reached the hill country again.

When I realized we were leaving the malarial coastlands and saw my first pine tree after that long, hot and difficult ordeal, I was so glad to be out of that mud and heat that I flung my arms around the tree and hugged it! The sun was still several degrees above the horizon, and we dragged ourselves to the town of Achuapa. The *comandante* happened to be an acquaintance of Hipolito's and received us cordially into his own home. I felt too bad to even eat, and went right to bed.

The following day Cam accepted the hospitality of an American mine official where he was served a hearty bowl of soup prepared by a Chinese chef, and all was well.

The first whiff of the soup put new life into me. And by the time I felt a good pressure on my belt, I had forgotten all my ailments.

On October 8, the weary colporteurs crossed back into Honduras and began their trek toward Comayaguela. The trails led them over hard, broken ground, across sterile plains, through forests of scrubby trees and across a river too deep to ford.

The boat was small. It had been carved out of a tough log and was seaworthy. First the men took our equipment across. Then they came back for the two mules. It was a beautiful sight – the little bark being pulled across the angry current by the hard-rowing oarsmen while on either side swam the snorting beasts and over all was shed the enchanting light of a tropical sunset.

Cam ended that little interlude by saying the boatman was interested in the gospel and offered to guide the men to his brother's farm where they could spend the night.

Four days later, after bathing in a creek and eating a hearty meal of beans and tortillas, Cam took part in a gospel meeting in the town of Oro-cuina. The singing had just begun when the local policeman came and ordered them to stop the meeting. "All public meetings have been prohibited throughout the republic." Cam noted, however, that the night before, the officials had closed their eyes to a small traveling circus performance.

October 7. I told the brethren to keep singing while I went to talk to the head of the police department. I told him that nearly all of the believers were in attendance at the meeting and that I was leaving in the morning, and it would be our last meeting for a while. Finally after further talking, he consented to our continuing. Hipolito gave a fine message.

> After what seemed an endless trip, Cam and Frisco arrived in Comayaguela, Honduras. Here Cam spent several days resting and regaining his strength at the home of his young missionary friends, the Lincolns. From here he wrote a most touching letter to his parents. As in some of the other letters, Cam only alluded to the hardships he and Frisco had encountered.

Comayaguela, Honduras
October 14, 1918

Dear Home Folks,

I arrived here last Thursday evening after a blessed trip across Nicaragua. With the exception of a week's illness at the home of a believer, we came through without a mishap. We had many sales, even though there is more poverty and much more sickness.

Here in Comayaguela they have had a plague of influenza. Many have died from it, but it's now easing up a bit. With the home-cooking I am getting at the Lincolns, my health has picked right up.

You can't imagine my joy when I found twenty letters waiting for me. I always read your letters last so didn't read the sad news of Carroll Byram's* death in

---

*Carroll Byram had been Cam's classmate and friend at Occidental College.

France until after I had read a very interesting letter from him, written while he was under fire. Until this war ends, I shall be afraid to open letters.

I have lost much more than a chum. He was like an elder brother to me. We were always happy in each other's company. We seemed to read each other's dispositions perfectly. We had always planned to travel together. In fact, he ended his last letter with, "Come and learn some French. We're getting along fine. After the war we'll visit old Spain. What do you say?"

Somehow I feel he died in my place and that I down here must do the work of two people. He gave his life for our country. I must give mine for our Lord. I am so glad I filled my last letter to him with spiritual things. Heaven now has an added attraction to me. His folks must feel so badly. I am going to write them this week.

Physical death is indeed sad, but how much sadder to think of the many soldiers who have not received spiritual life through faith in Christ. Let's all pray, send tracts, and in every way give a faithful testimony for our Lord.

I received a letter from Mr. Bishop. He wrote, "No doubt your taking up the Indian work will be a disappointment to Mr. Smith [secretary of the Los Angeles Bible House] and a loss to all of us at the Bible House. Yet seeing how God has used you for the salvation and enlightenment of a number of these Indians, and realizing that very few missionaries have the qualifications and background that would make possible a successful work among these Indians, I give my hearty approval to your future plans. I trust nothing will interfere or turn you away from them."

After this excerpt from Mr. Bishop's letter, Cam concluded with the news that he would shortly return to Guatemala City before taking up his new responsibilities in San Antonio. He also exhorted his brother Paul to finish his schooling before spending a year or two on the field.

Then without a paragraph break, in the middle of telling his parents how grateful he was for their prayers, he gave them a little reprimand that gives us further insight into the totality of the man who wanted to serve all people of whatever rank or station.

I received your letters of October 8, 15, 31, and November 9, 18 and 20. The only fault is that you gave me almost no election news. Did Randall get it? Who is governor? I am still interested in politics even though I am far from home, so let me know now and then.

Cam ended his letter with three Scripture references: Hebrews 10:37; III John 2 and II Corinthians 1:25.

True to his word and with renewed excitement about beginning a school for Indian children, Cam and Frisco headed southward toward the Honduran coast through El Salvador and then inland toward Guatemala City. Cam's letters and journal told of hardship trails similar to those he and Frisco had already endured.

He noted that all along the way he saw "evidences of the havoc wrought by the influenza people had nicknamed 'tronco' (heavy log), meaning that when a person gets the sickness, he feels as though he has been badly beaten."

He wrote about his own sadness at seeing a girl about twenty "lying dead stretched out in the middle of the floor of a poor hut with two women kneeling over her praying while pine chips burned as candles at each corner of the mat where the girl lay."

In the late afternoon of November 12, 1918, Cam and Frisco entered the town of San Miguel, El Salvador. It was here, after a long foot-weary journey, he learned the armistice had been signed. World War I had ended.

Guatemala City
December 19, 1918

Dear Home Folks,

We arrived last Saturday night after a great trip along the Pacific coast. It was the first time Frisco had seen the ocean. You should have seen the expression on his face! He said he was most fascinated with the breakers. I was too; it was great to dive into them. I went bathing twice a day. This gave me some relief from the terrible itch of the mosquito bites that have nearly driven me crazy.

There is a yellow fever epidemic on the coast that is about over, but the influenza is just now hitting Guatemala. All meetings have been prohibited.

I have an appointment for a conference with Mr. Bishop tomorrow to talk over arrangements for the school. I will be able to inform you more definitely of my plans when next I write.

Bushels of love,
Cameron
Psalm 23.

— 16 —

A TIME FOR LOVE

The tone of Cam's letter from Honduras had been one of good-natured spoofing, almost like the response of a preteen boy who thinks all girls are to be avoided like the plague.

> Comayaguela, Honduras
> August 15, 1918

...So Bob G. has gone and done it. The epidemic must be terrible up there. I have begun to wonder if it wouldn't be safer for me to join the army and go straight to France without stopping around home. There must be a regular man-catching campaign going on. Some letters I have received from my friends sound as though a good many of them want to come home on a month's furlough and arrange to get married. This is certainly not my desire at the moment.

If Cam was turning up his collar against the notion of marriage for himself, he perhaps should have given greater attention to the Apostle Paul's warning, "Anyone who thinks he is standing securely should take heed lest he fall" (1 Corinthians 10:12, paraphrase). The moment when Cam would fall was nearer than he realized. In his August letter, he had gently chided his friends for being so so "fickle," but he would only have a four-and a

half- month wait before he would enter what Eccles-
iastes 3:8 calls "a time for loving."

After that first Sunday dinner when she sang her
way into Robbie's heart, Cam saw Elvira Malmstrom only occasionally when he made a quick trip
through Guatemala City. The exception was
during the terrible days of the 1917 Christmas Day
earthquake when it seemed they ran into each
other every other day. However, he continued to be
a detached observer until two separate events altered his vision.

The first was a New Year's Day dinner. In Cam's
letter to his parents, they learned for the first time,
if they were able to read between the lines, that
their twenty-two-year-old son's thoughts blossomed with a heightened awareness of his own
humanity.

On New Year's Day I was invited over to the Allis-
sons' home for a feast. I was with a missionary, Miss
Malmstrom, who is looking after the printing press and
Mr. Allison's correspondence.

Admittedly there is little in these few short
words to suggest that Cam was doing anything
more than merely supplying his parents with a
piece of information about Elvira Malmstrom's
missionary duties, But to know Cam's mind is to
know he rarely did anything or wrote about anything that hadn't first captivated his attention. Six
days later, with an eagerness that exploded off the
page, Cam, while not mentioning Elvira's name,
clearly had succumbed to an ecstasy of ardent love.

Antigua, Guatemala
January 12, 1919

Dear Home Folks,

My! This has been a wonderful day! Our God is able!
Nothing is too difficult for Him! When we turn our-

selves over into His hands, with one behind, He shoves us on, and with the other before, He opens the way. My joy in Him is so great that I can hardly contain it and words are far too weak to express it! I can just shout with the Psalmist, "Bless the Lord O my soul and all that is within me, bless His Holy Name."

Cam had returned to Guatemala City in December with every intention of bringing his dream of a school for Indian children into reality. Unfortunately, the siege of influenza was affecting nearly everyone in the country. So serious was the epidemic that the government ordered everyone to wear guaze masks, and coffee beans spoiled on the bushes for lack of people to harvest them. Cam wrote that in view of this terrible ordeal, he would have to postpone his school plans for several months.

In the meantime I plan to spend my time studying the Bible and Spanish, and doing evangelistic work among the Cakchiquel people. I have also discovered the believers need simple Bible teaching more than they need preaching. This is important if they are ever to grow in their spiritual lives.

I find it is going to be very difficult at present to thoroughly evangelize the Cakchiquel people without utilizing their own language. Thus I plan to start a study of the language right away. Actually I have already started with the hope of being able to teach the Bible to them in their own language. I realize this is going to be difficult because there is no one who can explain the grammar to me.

When things settle down [after the influenza is over], I know enough funds will come in to start the school.

Already Mr. Bishop has promised the school a cow and a calf. One of the local missionaries has promised twenty-five dollars, and two others have pledged five dollars each. Frisco and I have nearly thirty dollars from our sales commissions, and you, my dear parents, have sent $47.50. I have nearly a hundred dollars of my own, besides what the Indians are going to do. So at this point, finances are the least of my worries. When I need more, the Lord will send it in as long as I spend it wisely.

Anyone who knew Cam understood he meant to do exactly what he felt God leading him to do. In an earlier letter, he had asked his brother-in-law Fleet, to send down a complete set of carpenter's hand tools. He already had a two-man cross-cut saw and was trying to get some of the Cakchiquel men to handsaw lumber for a chapel.

True to his vision, Cam had sent out letters asking for a professional teacher to come and join him in his venture. He and Frisco were preparing for a large flower and vegetable garden. Any day he was expecting a parcel from home containing a variety of garden seeds. He had requested early sugar and field corn, Kentucky Wonder beans, lima beans, and black-eyed beans. He had sent letters to the government asking how to go about receiving agricultural assistance from them. Specifically, he wanted the best variety of grape and fig cuttings plus any seeds they might suggest for the Antigua area. He also wondered about olive seeds, "if olives are grown without budding."

With the exception of one slight problem, everything was running according to plan. The problem Cam hadn't yet resolved was the question of land.

In an effort to involve the government in his school project, he approached the head man in charge of land development for Antigua. He was cordially received and given a promise that the governor would look into the matter.

In a letter home, Cam also disclosed his struggle with another problem. Two Cakchiquel Indian believers opposed the whole idea of a school.

Antigua, Guatemala
January 20, 1919

Dear Home Folks,

The work goes on about the same. The devil is still plenty active, but faith triumphs over all. I think the greatest difficulty I have had with this school project has come from the well-to-do Indian men, Catarino and Julian. They have opposed the idea giving as their reason that it will cost too much money. The other reason for their opposition is that they feel the non-believers will persecute them too much.

Last week I had prayer and a heart-to-heart talk with Catarino, and while we prayed, the Lord completely broke down his miserliness. The result was a promise from him to help with the school. However, several days later it seems he again lost his courage and wanted me to wait for another year to put up the school.

Later I told the two men about Gideon and also about the men of faith listed in Hebrews, chapter eleven. However, Catarino didn't want to put on his spectacles of faith. He had greatly discouraged the other brethren. Yet, he still may help when he sees us going ahead with the plans.

Speaking of plans, Mr. Bishop requested that Cam outline a statement of purpose for himself and the school. Since Cam's mother had requested almost the same information, he gave her the same outline as he had given Mr. Bishop.

Antigua, Guatemala
February 1, 1919

Dear Home Folks,

So that you will understand my purpose and plans for the school, I will give you the same outline that I gave to Mr. Bishop. They are:

I. I feel called to work among the Cakchiquel Indians of Guatemala, most of whom live within the territory worked by the Central American Mission. Although I feel called primarily to the Indians and shall devote most of my time to them, I shall not fail to evangelize the Ladino populations as opportunity permits.

II. I intend to work in perfect harmony with the Central American Mission. As yet, the Lord has not made it clear that I should apply for membership. However, whatever congregations I am able to organize in the territory will belong to them. I shall in every way try to comply with their wishes and shall practically be one of their workers, except that I shall not look to them for support. If the Lord should so direct, I would consider it a blessed privilege to belong to a mission I so highly regard as the Central American Mission.

III. My work is to be predominantly evangelistic and Bible teaching (in the Indian language).

IV. I also plan to direct a day school in the town of San Antonio (ten miles from Antigua). I do not expect to do any of the teaching myself. Believers' children from neighboring towns will be received, provided they can be taken care of. No tuition will be charged for children of believers. At present we plan to have only two grades. Our future plans are to give no more than a five-year course.

V. If it is true that the Central American Mission does not look with favor upon mission industrial schools, I will limit my efforts in that line to agricultural training and as much carpentry, etc., as is necessary to good farming. Most of the Indians among whom I work are farmers, and I will be merely helping them in their present industry. Certainly if I live the doctrine I teach, I must help them in their material welfare at least this much.

At present I shall have to do most of the practical teaching, and I shall let it take little more of my time than what I would want for my outdoor recreation.

I hope to get a few acres on the outskirts of San Antonio to serve as school, farm, and to also raise food for the cow and mule we already have. Five acres would be desirable, but this is something for the future.

VI. I have decided that if the Lord permits, I will stay on the field till the close of this school year, October 1919. Although I would like to take a course in some Bible institute before getting deeper into the work, it is probable that I shall stay on the field two or three more years before returning to the States for study.

VII. I have no promised source of support except that of Joshua 1:9: "Have I not commanded thee? Be strong and of good courage; be not afraid; neither be dismayed; for the Lord thy God is with thee whithersoever thou goest."

Cam concluded his letter to his parents with an earnest prayer request.

We now have a mule, a cow, a calf, and a pig, but as yet we haven't even a lot to keep them on. Pray that the Lord will send in funds to buy a little tract of land, even though it be only an acre.

The rest of the school supplies I ordered have arrived,

so that as soon as the influenza passes, we plan to open the school.

Lovingly in Philippians 1:3
Cameron.

It was in the midst of all these wonderful dreams that Cam experienced the second event that altered his regard for Elvira. He was stricken with a severe case of malaria.

In late December 1918, Cam had relinquished his duties as colporteur with the Los Angeles Bible House. He was now a fully independent missionary living in Antigua. And it was here he had taken ill and had been cared for by the mother of a local Ladino pastor. During his recuperation, Elvira, who was on an extended visit to a missionary in Antigua, took time each day to visit and encourage the severely ill Cam Townsend.

Thus in the space of a few short weeks, Cam had moved forward into the wonders and hazards of a dynamic, loving relationship.

I am just the happiest fellow on earth. My love for Elvira grows greater every day, and hers for me. I didn't know I was capable of such great love.

With a special romantic flair, William Cameron Townsend proposed to Elvira Malmstrom on Valentine's Day, February 14, 1919. Unknown to Cam at the time, only a few days earlier, Elvira had received a letter of proposal from his good friend Robbie. But three days later Elvira made her choice and wrote Cam's parents.

Antigua, Guatemala
February 17, 1919

Dear Mother and Father Townsend,
It does not at all seem strange to write to you dear

folks, even though I have not had the pleasure of meeting you face to face for Cameron has told me such lovely things about his beloved parents and family. I am looking forward to the day when I shall be able to meet you face to face, should the Lord tarry.

I do not know how to express in words the joy that has come into my heart, and as Cameron says, "It is so sweet because it is all of the Lord."

I can well understand there must be certain anxious feelings in your hearts about the welfare and happiness of Cameron, since he is so far from home and living under abnormal conditions in a strange country. However, I want to assure you that with all that lies within my power, I long to make him the happiest boy in the world, with a desire, especially, of being a true, spiritual companion.

I feel that Cameron and I are engaged in such a wonderful work, and it is most important as the time is short and because there are so many around us who live in utter spiritual darkness. My earnest prayer is that with the deep love in our hearts for one another, God may continue to fill our hearts with more love for Him and a passion and compassion for the lost as we have never known before. Thus our efforts will not be in vain.

I pray also our home life will be a blessed one. "Not by might, nor by power, but by my Spirit, saith the Lord of Hosts."

I only wish I were there with you to put my arms around you instead of having to write a cold, formal letter. However, believe me to be, your loving little daughter,

Elvira Malmstrom

In the course of her regular stenographic duties for the Presbyterian mission, Elvira had to write

Rev. Paul Burgess who, on March 2, 1919, was in Greeley, Colorado. At the end of her letter she wrote:

Now I have a surprise for you and Mrs. Burgess. Mr. Cameron Townsend and I are engaged and hope to be united in marriage sometime this year.* I think you know Cameron and what a fine Christian young man he is. You perhaps know that during this past year he traveled through all Central America with the exception of the republic of Costa Rica, and has had a wonderful opportunity of becoming acquainted with the people and customs of these countries. We both feel called to work among the Indians. Right now our hearts are with the Cakchiquel Indians, and we are asking the Lord to definitely direct us as to just where He would have us settle down.

With kind Christian greetings to you and Mrs. Burgess and the girls.

Sincerely,
Elvira Malmstrom

Cam's feelings about his engagement are recorded in a letter home. This incomplete letter is perhaps the sole surviving record of his thoughts prior to his July 9 wedding. He confesses his deep feelings for Elvira with an amazing candor and further confesses that since he had stopped his daily travels, has found it hard to find anything to write about. "I am letting my letters take the place of my diary."

---

*The date was later set for July 9, Cam's birthday. Cam wanted to be married on his birthday as his father had been married on his birthday.

Antigua, Guatemala
February 19, 1919

Dear Home Folks,

Say Paul, could you get down in time to serve as my best man? The sweetest girl on earth (step back Ethel and take second place!) thinks that you would make a dandy.

I tell you, folks, I've met lots of fine girls in my travels among the different mission stations down here, but never have I met a girl to compare with the one that stole my heart last New Year's Day. I have mentioned Mr. Allison's assistant, Elvira Malmstrom, in several of my letters but haven't said more as I was waiting to know whether she returned the love I have for her before writing my beloved folks in detail. But last Friday, Valentine's Day, I wooed and won (veni, vidi, vici) and now on the first mail I am writing my folks about the wonderful treasure that has come into my life.

My! How you will love her when you get to know her! She is so sweet and altogether lovely. I can just see how her precious blue eyes and happy smile will win your hearts even as they have won mine.

Whenever I have thought of picking out a life companion, I have always thought of how she would please first my Lord, and second my home folks. Well my darling Elvira fills both bills perfectly. She is the most spiritual girl I think I have ever known. Her very presence draws me closer to the Lord. How I enjoy studying the Bible and praying with her. We are truly one in the Lord!

Although Elvira didn't arrive on the field until about two months before Rob and I did, she has already come to be Mr. Allison's mainstay in the publishing house office and evangelistic work. You would think from this that she is one of those mannish girls, but she isn't. She is a delightfully girlish little girl.

She sings so sweetly and is an artist on the piano. She can write two hundred shorthand words a minute, and when she was working as a stenographer in Chicago, she rattled the keys in proportion. Her business education will make up for my lack in that line.

In every way we make a perfect match. Oh, I could fill several pages telling you all about what a wonder she is – how quickly she learned Spanish, how she looks after Mr. Allison's work in his absence, how she loves the Indians, and how she loves to tell people about Jesus. But I haven't time. Some day you will know her, and to know her is to love her. And best of all, she loves me as I love her, if that is possible.

And say, Fleet, I'm not so slow after all. New Year's Day was the first time I ever went to call on her, and in six weeks I had won her. But it was a work of the Lord, pure and simple, and I have never had a minute's doubt as to His will in the matter.

Our plans are very indefinite. She is supported by the Moody Church of Chicago and they want her to take a furlough, resting and speaking about the work. . . .

The remainder of this letter is lost to history. However, whatever indecisions Cam faced on February 19 were all resolved by his wedding day on July 9. Rev. Paul Burgess helped supply part of the missing link in a letter he wrote a day or so after performing the wedding.

"On our way down to Guatemala from Colorado, we met Carl Malmstrom, brother of Elvira, Mr. Allison's stenographer. He was on his way to attend her wedding. This took place while we were here and was a very happy affair. The newlyweds are scheduled to work in Antigua (they will live in San Antonio) and will work under the Central American Mission."

While Paul Burgess had described the wedding as a pretty and happy occasion, Elvira, of course, esteemed it as the most beautiful she had ever seen. In a letter addressed to the Central American Bulletin, she provided a more complete insight into that most important of days.

Antigua, Guatemala
August 30, 1919

As you know, for special doings in this country, they send immense floral pieces like we see at a funeral home. However, I think the idea of showering flowers for the living is a great deal more beautiful. You can perhaps get a small idea of what a beautiful sight the church was that night with about a dozen immense floral pieces on the platform. Besides other smaller baskets and bouquets, the entire church was decorated with palm ferns and flowers.

After the wedding ceremony, my class of girls sang a song and one of the Bible women spoke. [It was one such woman who had made Elvira's stunning white dress. And not to be outdone, Luther Rees, president of the Central American Mission, had given Cam fifty dollars to buy himself a new wedding suit. Another missionary, A.B. Treichler, gave Cam a $2.50 gold piece which Cam had a jeweler make into Elvira's wedding band.]

On Thursday morning we took the stage for Antigua. We arrived at our new home about four o'clock. How surprised I was to find such a darling home and everything arranged so tastefully. Surely our joy is complete in Him.

Cam and Elvira spent their first night together in the home of a missionary, and the following morning, Elvira's brother Carl (who was Cam's best man because Paul couldn't make it), joined the bride and groom on their bouncy ride to Antigua.

Only one thing marred Cam's joy. Just before the wedding he learned that Frisco, his beloved friend and colleague, had been stricken with malaria and died. This severe blow was the first of several blows that would lead to Cam's wilderness experience.

Cam and Elvira's work with the Cakchiquel Indians eventually led to Cam's completion of the Cakchiquel New Testament in 1931 and his commitment to worldwide Bible translation. A second volume of Cam's writings entitled, "The Middle Years," covering the period between Cam's marriage and the formation of SIL and WBT, is currently being compiled. It is hoped that this companion volume will give further insight into the man called "Uncle Cam."